"*Compassion (&) Conviction* provides a reconciliatory prescription for a political environment infected by discord, animus, and extremism. This book stands as a clarion call for a movement founded on the principle that every human being carries the image of God and driven by a passion to do justice and change the world. This is not just a must-read, this is a must-do!"

Samuel Rodriguez, president of the National Hispanic Christian Leadership Conference, lead pastor of New Season Christian Worship Center, Sacramento, California

"The book *Compassion (&) Conviction: The AND Campaign's Guide to Faithful Civic Engagement* is a much-needed text that skillfully guides believers on how to exercise their civic duties without compromise. The authors assert that people of faith have a moral obligation to demonstrate love for our neighbors by weighing in on political matters, yet we should also respect and work constructively with nonbelievers. If ever there was a time for people of faith to love others while standing up for what is right, that time is now. This book offers a framework and guidance on how to civically live out your faith."

John K. Jenkins Sr., pastor of First Baptist Church of Glenarden, Maryland

"I love the AND Campaign because they are trying to raise the voice of Jesus in a world that is often us versus them, red versus blue, elephant versus donkey. In a time marked by division, this timely book raises an urgent question: *What does the Bible say?* I believe that faith can and should impact our cultural and civic engagement. I pray that you are informed and challenged by the thoughts and exercises in *Compassion (&) Conviction.* We need this message now more than ever."

Nick Hall, founder and chief communicator for PULSE, author of *Reset*

"At a time when America's body of Christ is as divided as our nation itself, the AND Campaign has presented a much-needed model for those who aspire to stay true to biblical principles—all of them!—in their civic engagement. Free of partisanship and cultural bias, this book provides a framework that, if adhered to, could lead to unity, healing, and perhaps even revival. Just in the nick of time, the AND Campaign has given us a gem, a light, a guide for how Bible believers can accurately represent Christ in a public square so desperately in need of our true and faithful witness."

Chris Broussard, broadcaster for FOX Sports, founder and president of the K.I.N.G. Movement

"*Compassion (&) Conviction* is an outstanding tool in sharing the consistent, courageous, and faith-filled message of the AND Campaign. At a time when too many Christians let their politics shape their faith, this book is an example of faith shaping politics. You don't have to agree with every word in this book, but we should be grateful for the biblical principles and moral analysis that make this resource so timely and challenging. Justin Giboney, Michael Wear, and Chris Butler offer a path to faithful citizenship in tough times."

John Carr, director of the Initiative on Catholic Social Thought and Public Life at Georgetown University

"People commonly lament our age's political division and tribalism. Some have lived at the poles of political discourse, and they've forgotten their way back to a commonly shared center. Finding our way back to one another can only happen if we learn not to bifurcate our politics. We need a movement to reunite ourselves, reunite with our neighbors, and reunite political ideals that never should have been divided in the first place. That reunion will feel like a strange new land for many us, so we need guides, pathways, tools, and discipline for talking and working together for the common good. You hold in your hands a creative struggle for wholeness, just the kind of help we need in our age."

Thabiti M. Anyabwile, pastor of Anacostia River Church, Washington, DC

"Empowering. Practical. Enlightening. Convicting. Finally here's a resource for Christians to understand their civil duty in voting and how they should engage in political affairs. We've gone far too long without a professionally detailed resource that answers our specific controversies such as our involvement as Christians in politics, our engagement in social justice without compromising our faith, and our dedication to justice. This book isn't just an explanation of our Christian duty in the public space; it's an invitation to actively engage in politics and civics as informed believers. This resource must be taught, used, and circulated locally and abroad. Our republic depends on it."

Cornelius Lindsey, lead pastor of the Gathering Oasis Church, Atlanta

COMPASSION

CONVICTION

THE AND CAMPAIGN'S GUIDE
TO FAITHFUL CIVIC ENGAGEMENT

**JUSTIN GIBONEY, MICHAEL WEAR,
AND CHRIS BUTLER**

**FOREWORD BY
BARBARA WILLIAMS-SKINNER**

An imprint of InterVarsity Press
Downers Grove, Illinois

InterVarsity Press
P.O. Box 1400, Downers Grove, IL 60515-1426
ivpress.com
email@ivpress.com

InterVarsity Press® is the book-publishing division of InterVarsity Christian Fellowship/USA®, a movement of students and faculty active on campus at hundreds of universities, colleges, and schools of nursing in the United States of America, and a member movement of the International Fellowship of Evangelical Students. For information about local and regional activities, visit intervarsity.org.

All Scripture quotations, unless otherwise indicated, are taken from The Holy Bible, New International Version®, NIV®. Copyright © 1973, 1978, 1984, 2011 by Biblica, Inc.™ Used by permission of Zondervan. All rights reserved worldwide. www.zondervan.com. The "NIV" and "New International Version" are trademarks registered in the United States Patent and Trademark Office by Biblica, Inc.™

While any stories in this book are true, some names and identifying information may have been changed to protect the privacy of individuals.

Cover design and image composite: David Fassett
Interior design: Daniel van Loon
Cover image: © Rafa Elias / Moment Collection / Getty Images

ISBN 978-0-8308-4810-2 (print)
ISBN 978-0-8308-4811-9 (digital)

Printed in the United States of America ♾

InterVarsity Press is committed to ecological stewardship and to the conservation of natural resources in all our operations. This book was printed using sustainably sourced paper.

Library of Congress Cataloging-in-Publication Data
A catalog record for this book is available from the Library of Congress.

| P | 23 | 22 | 21 | 20 | 19 | 18 | 17 | 16 | 15 | 14 | 13 | 12 | 11 | 10 | 9 | 8 | 7 | 6 | 5 | 4 | 3 | 2 | 1 |
| Y | 37 | 36 | 35 | 34 | 33 | 32 | 31 | 30 | 29 | 28 | 27 | 26 | 25 | 24 | 23 | 22 | 21 | 20 |

THIS BOOK IS DEDICATED TO

Dr. Albertine Marshall

a mentor and dedicated Christian educator.

CONTENTS

FOREWORD

BARBARA WILLIAMS-SKINNER

As the 2020 presidential election process nears, our country's political climate will require Christians to faithfully, prayerfully, and thoughtfully engage others with a focus on promoting social justice, guided by moral order. The good news is that you are holding in your hand a life-changing book. This remarkable guide serves as a solid framework for Christians to engage in the political process in a faithful, informed, and effective manner without sacrificing deeply held, biblically based convictions.

For many of us, religion and politics are deeply intertwined. Does the separation between church and state imply that there should be a separation between religion and politics? Between morality and government? What is the relationship between my Christianity (or my commitment to the teachings of Jesus) and my politics? Where does one end and the other begin? These are hard questions, ones that *Compassion (&) Conviction* help us to address in a spirit of humility and love.

Never before have so many followers of Jesus Christ had more difficulty in the (too often negative) way we relate to those whose views differ from our own on hot-button issues such as abortion, same-sex marriage, racial equality, immigration, and the environment. Without question, there is a growing political divide in our country. Yet as Christians we are expected to engage in both private and public spaces in ways that honor God, consistent with the great commands in Matthew 22:37-39 to love God and to love our neighbors as ourselves.

Exercising faith in these challenging times takes courage. Although Christians are still called to speak truth in an increasingly corrupt world, it is vital that we think carefully about how our faith informs our politics. We must hold fast to God's declaration in Genesis 1:27 that every person is made in his image. And we can practice this truth in ways that will not diminish human dignity. Just as we have received God's immeasurable grace, we should be ready to extend grace to those we disagree with, something I consider even timelier for Christ followers today.

Whether you're a Christian or non-Christian, it can be challenging to show that kindness to those who hold a radically different worldview. Showing kindness means being able to unconditionally accept people for who they are without approving of their choices, even if we believe those choices are outside of God's will according to our understanding of God's Word. With the guidance provided through *Compassion (&) Conviction*, we can learn how Christ-centered political engagement can be delivered in a loving and caring way.

May God use this book to awaken his people with a vision for the good of all Americans—a vision that is not fully represented in either party's platform—by providing us with a key to unlock doors where other keys have failed.

PREFACE

E very Christian in America is political. This is unavoidable.
It is the privilege and burden of citizenship. We can choose
to not exercise the duties of citizenship, but that does not mean
we do not have them. People are paying attention to how Christians operate in political life. They want to know if faith makes
a difference in how to think about politics, in how to carry out
those duties of citizenship. Christians, too, are asking how their
faith ought to impact their political outlook. We believe that
how we answer this question can glorify God, bless our nation
and our neighbors, and affirm that the gospel we proclaim is real
and meaningful for all of life.

The AND Campaign's leadership team created this resource
to help believers engage the civic space as faithful Christians and
informed citizens. Our organizational mission is to educate and
organize Christians for civic and cultural engagement that re-
sults in better representation, more just and compassionate
policies, and a healthier political culture.

While traveling around the nation speaking to pastors,
Christian educators, and people in the pews, it has become clear
to us that many Christians are searching for a better understanding of the civic process and the role our faith should play
in it (if any role at all). We found that some believers were

intimidated by the civic space while others had allowed it to compromise their beliefs or ruin personal relationships. We even heard a story about congregants physically fighting in a church about political differences. We resolved to bring clarity to the proper intersection of faith and politics—a subject that could greatly benefit or harm believers and the world as a whole. This book is a concrete expression of our resolve.

We came to this effort as Christians with strong biblical convictions and a wealth of experience in the sociopolitical arena. Whether working for a US president, managing state and local campaigns, pastoring, or advocating for better education policy, we have seen close up how faith can provide direction or be misdirected in the political realm. Through successes and failures, study and practice—but mostly by applying Jesus' teachings and sound biblical doctrine—we've developed a gospel-centered framework to help Christians reflect the compassion and conviction of Jesus Christ in the public square. We are not telling Christians who to vote for or implying that we must agree on every issue; rather, we're providing a framework for Christian Democrats, Republicans, and Independents to engage in a more faithful, informed, and effective manner.

CHAPTER ONE

CHRISTIANS

POLITICS

I n 1830, the Indian Removal Act led to what's known as the Trail of Tears, in which almost fifty thousand indigenous people were removed from the southeastern United States and relocated west of the Mississippi River. More than four thousand persons died from disease, hunger, and cold during the journey. This forced relocation was popular with Americans who were eligible to vote because it freed up land for settlers, but it led America further down the path toward the heinous sin of exploitation and oppression of indigenous people.[1]

According to Robert L. Burgdorf Jr., who contracted polio as a toddler, people with disabilities faced "widespread, systemic, inhumane discrimination" prior to organizing and advocating alongside their allies against such societal barriers. Children with disabilities were systematically excluded from public schools; public transportation was almost totally inaccessible to those with mobility and visual impairments; and many were institutionalized in remote, unsanitary, and dangerously overcrowded facilities. Some people with mental and physical conditions faced involuntary sterilization and were denied lifesaving medication and medical treatment. All these things motivated Burgdorf to write the Americans with Disabilities Acts of 1990.[2] This landmark legislation prohibited discrimination against people with disabilities in employment, public services, public accommodations, and telecommunication.[3]

Both instances represent political decisions that changed the course of history. In one instance, Americans failed to stand up for the voiceless and vulnerable. In the latter example, America finally corrected a history of injustice and neglect. In both cases, citizens had an opportunity to significantly affect the present and future well-being of others. Had Christians organized and rallied against the Indian Removal Act, perhaps they could've stopped President Andrew Jackson from signing it, saved thousands of lives, and even improved the station of indigenous people today. We'll never know for sure, but we do know that our participation in the political process or lack thereof—and the principles we employ—greatly affect our neighbors.

Politics can be a matter of freedom or imprisonment, free speech or censorship, housing or homelessness, life or death. Politics is an essential aspect of modern life. It is how we govern ourselves, and it plays a major role in how we organize ourselves as a society. Political actions have started wars and defined certain people as property, but they've also fed the hungry and provided care for the sick. Christians must be faithful and thoughtful in how we choose to wield our influence and political power.

We hear endlessly about political scandals, broken campaign promises, deceptions, and power trips. Watch local news and it immediately becomes clear that politics can be corrupt, dangerous, and filled with idols. Some people get involved in politics for the wrong reasons, and others who start with lofty ideals seem to lose their original purpose in the fray. Given this reality, should Christians participate in politics? Should we partake in such a broken arena or leave the political world to its own devices?

Politics is ugly and imperfect because our world is broken—because we as individuals are broken. Nothing was unaffected by the fall (Genesis 3), and politics is no exception. But like it or not, politics touches every aspect of society. How and when we worship, what constitutes a crime, and what children learn in school are all subject to political decisions. To avoid or dismiss political engagement is to forgo an important opportunity to help our neighbors and to promote the righteousness and justice that are the foundation of God's throne (Psalm 89:14).

We hear a lot of disheartening stories about politics and politicians, but there are also many encouraging stories—stories in which the needy are supported and society is improved because of kindhearted advocacy and thoughtful policy decisions. Refusing to engage civically is failing to steward the things God has placed in our sphere of influence. How can we be salt and light if we have no contact with society (Matthew 5:13-16)—especially in an arena with such a significant and broad impact on society? Christians should engage politics because doing so provides us with a robust opportunity to love our neighbor by acting justly, promoting human flourishing, and seeking the prosperity of our community.

The Christian's Primary Objective

As Christians, our primary objective is to profess the gospel of Jesus Christ to all nations (Matthew 28:16-20). No other task should be allowed to interfere with or obscure that purpose. If the Great Commission becomes secondary, or if Christianity is understood primarily as a means of accomplishing social or political goals, then we've handed to Caesar what belongs to God (Matthew 22:21).

Do not interpret this book's focus on the political space as a suggestion that professing the gospel should be subordinated to political activity. While God has given us power to bring about change and help those around us in real ways (James 2:15-16), our world will continue to be a place of sin and suffering until Jesus returns (Romans 8:19-21). This truth is important to keep in mind as we discuss our interactions with society. It provides us with perspective, helping us remember the ultimate things rather than being consumed by the temporal matters of this world. Our civic participation will not glorify God if it's placed above worship, evangelism, or Christian fellowship.

Why Should Christians Engage Politics?

What are you willing to do for the people you love? If a family member was being mistreated, in addition to your prayers would you also use your time and resources to stop them from being hurt? If they were unjustly imprisoned, would you advocate for them? If a teacher was treating your child unfairly, would you address the issue? Of course you would. We rightly expect that kind of urgent action from the people who say they care about us.

In the Great Commandment, Jesus says to "love the Lord your God with all your heart and with all your soul and with all your mind" and to "love your neighbor as yourself" (Matthew 22:37-39). When Jesus is asked "Who is my neighbor?" by a lawyer who's trying to narrow this love imperative, Jesus responds with the Good Samaritan parable. Through that illustration we learn that our neighbors aren't just allies or people in our community. Anyone can be our neighbor, and we are called to be a neighbor to everyone we have the capacity and occasion to help (Luke 10:25-37). To love others as we love ourselves is to give them the care and consideration that we'd provide for ourselves and our loved ones. If we were negatively impacted by injustice, we would advocate for ourselves; according to Scripture, we should also advocate and stand up for others (Isaiah 1:17).

Part of taking the Great Commandment seriously is realizing that love is more than a feeling or sentiment. Love is substantive and active. Loving our neighbors is not the same as simply not hating them; in the biblical sense love is not a lack of hate or of anything else. Love has form and content, as described in Scripture, and it compels us to act (1 Corinthians 13; see also Matthew 5:43-47). If you never left your home and avoided all interaction with other people, you couldn't be characterized as a loving person. Instead, you might even be unloving because of your lack of concern for others.

Loving our neighbors involves actively seeking their well-being. James 2:15-17 illustrates this point well:

Suppose a brother or a sister is without clothes and daily food. If one of you says to them, "Go in peace; keep warm and well fed," but does nothing about their physical needs, what good is it? In the same way, faith by itself, if it is not accompanied by action, is dead.

Saying that we love our neighbors is nonsense if it's not reflected in our actions. Such actions are the outworking of our faith. If we're unwilling to go out of our way and use our resources to make sure others are taken care of, we're not living like the good Samaritan—or, more importantly, like Jesus Christ.

The Great Requirement and Doing Justice

In Micah 6:8, we find what has been called the Great Requirement:

He has shown you, O mortal, what is good.
 And what does the LORD require of you?
To act justly and to love mercy
 and to walk humbly with your God.

Just as the Great Commandment requires us to actively love our neighbors, the Great Requirement commands us to further the cause of justice.

The first part of this requirement, "act justly," obligates believers to take affirmative steps toward promoting justice. Like love, justice is more than merely the lack of injustice. Justice is substantive and active; it means we're willing to give of ourselves for others. The political arena enables Christians to act justly in meaningful ways.

The prophet Isaiah describes God as a purveyor of righteousness and justice continually, and speaks to God's expectation that his children will bring about righteousness and justice as well (Isaiah 59:14-17). Justice is a clear and prominent theme in the Old and New Testaments. Also, in both the Old and New Testament, Scripture tells us that government is ordained by God. Paul writes in Romans, "Let everyone be subject to the governing authorities, for there is no authority except that which God has established. The authorities that exist have been established by God" (Romans 13:1). Government is for our good (Romans 13:4), and there is a biblical expectation that governmental bodies ought to uphold and advance justice (Amos 5:15). The Psalms contain a prayer that governmental leaders of that time might "defend the afflicted among the people, save the children of the needy," and "crush the oppressor" (Psalm 72:4).

In other words, our government is tasked by God with protecting us and rendering justice. Moreover, while there is no biblical prescription for precisely which system of government (monarchy, liberal democracy, etc.) is best, we can trust that God has placed us in a particular time, place, and context in which political decisions regularly affect our neighbors for good and for ill. Therefore, Christians should participate in the political system and do our best to ensure that society is treating people fairly and upholding healthy standards of human dignity. In Jeremiah 29:7, God calls the believer to "seek the peace and prosperity of the city to which I have carried you into exile. Pray to the LORD for it, because if it prospers, you too will prosper." We're not islands unto ourselves; we're affected by what goes on around us and should pray and take action out of concern for it.

Whether we're protecting the unborn, supporting fair prison sentences, or making sure the elderly are taken care of, politics provides a forum for advocating for our neighbor's well-being and pursuing justice. Our daily walk should be a promotion of the love and truth of the gospel (Ephesians 4:15). Treating all God's children with human dignity through the political arena is an opportunity we should not bypass.

Politics provides Christians with an opportunity to actively love our neighbors through advocacy, policymaking, and civic representation. To refuse to engage in politics is to refuse to take advantage of a useful tool for God's work.

BIBLICAL EXAMPLES

Christians aren't limited to analyzing our relationship with the public square solely in theory or through abstract application. The Bible itself provides us with several concrete examples of righteous people who used politics to further the will of God and help their neighbors.

Joseph *(Genesis 39–41)*

After Joseph's brothers sold him into slavery in Egypt and he was imprisoned for a crime he didn't commit, Joseph was asked to interpret Pharaoh's dream (Genesis 37:18-26; 39:2–40:23; 41:14-24). After successfully interpreting dreams for Pharaoh, Joseph was considered a man of discernment and wisdom, and he was put in charge of the whole land of Egypt (Genesis 41:39-40). This was a government position of great authority that forced Joseph to make some tough political decisions. Joseph traveled around Egypt to understand the lay of the land and familiarize himself with the job he had undertaken (Genesis 41:46). He created a strategy and processes for surviving the famine. During the seven years of abundance, he collected all the food produced and stored it (Genesis 41:47-48). When the seven years of famine began, Egypt was able to survive it because of Joseph's plan (Genesis 41:56-57). They were also able to sell grain to famished people from other areas.

Moses *(Exodus 5–12)*

After growing up in Pharaoh's family and later choosing to embrace his Hebrew heritage, Moses was chosen by God to deliver his people out of slavery (Exodus 2:23-25; 3:7-9). Moses was hesitant to accept his commission because he thought he was inadequate. As part of his commission he had to confront Pharaoh and attempt to convince him to release the Hebrews from captivity. In essence, Moses was using his influence to try to persuade Pharaoh to do as God commanded, which was by definition a political act, although it had far greater implications. He also had to deal with the complaints of his people once Pharaoh increased their labor due to Moses' demands (Exodus 5:21). Moses' faith in

God and his willingness to confront government authorities on God's behalf resulted in the liberation of the Hebrews.

Daniel *(Daniel 1–2, 6)*

After King Nebuchadnezzar besieged Jerusalem, he took its most talented young people and brought them into his Babylonian kingdom (Daniel 1). Daniel was one of the young people the king tried to endear and indoctrinate so they would follow him uncritically. But Daniel stood up to the king on more than one occasion. First, he refused to defile himself by drinking the king's wine or by eating his meat (Daniel 1:8). He also refused to stop praying to God when an ordinance required him to do so (Daniel 6:10-22). Furthermore, Daniel worked with the king by interpreting his dreams and was given "a high position" as "ruler over the entire province of Babylon and placed in charge of all its wise men" (Daniel 2:48). When faced with political pressure, Daniel refused to defile himself, but he didn't refuse to accept a political position from which he could do good for others.

Ezra and Nehemiah *(Ezra 1:1-11; Nehemiah 1:1–7:3)*

Ezra and Nehemiah were central figures in Israel's return from Babylonian exile. Ezra worked with the Persian king to rebuild the temple in Jerusalem "to fulfill the word of the LORD spoken by Jeremiah" (Ezra 1:1), and Nehemiah worked to rebuild the wall (Nehemiah 2:17-18). Neither man could have accomplished his task without engaging government and the public square. Both men endured discouragement and political opposition that was determined to prevent them from doing a "great project" for God (Nehemiah 6:3; see also Ezra 4:8-24; Nehemiah 4). They both persevered and advocated to continue with God's work. They used secular government and political mechanisms to do God's business.

Paul *(Acts 16:37-39)*

Paul was a Roman citizen, and he used his citizenship—a political designation—to further his God-given commission. After being beaten by government authorities in Philippi, he informed them that he was a Roman citizen (Acts 16:37). This was a major revelation that forced them to let him go, but he wouldn't accept a secret release. Paul made them escort him out of the city to make a public statement that would give the Philippian church some relief and encouragement (Acts 16:38-40). Instead of using his political influence for self-preservation and his own benefit, he used it to further the mission of the church.

HISTORICAL EXAMPLES

There are also many historical examples of Christians faithfully using political means to fight for justice and righteousness.

William Wilberforce: *Politician and Abolitionist*

William Wilberforce was born in the United Kingdom in 1759. He was raised in a wealthy family and his strong connections helped him achieve his political ambitions early in life. In 1780, he was elected to Parliament and would serve until 1852. Wilberforce converted to evangelical Christianity during England's religious revival in 1785, and his faith was the catalyst for his great passion to end slavery. He and a group of abolitionists known as the "Clapham Sect" committed themselves to ending slavery in the United Kingdom and pursued that objective through petitions, propaganda, and organizing. Wilberforce's goal of ending slavery was achieved in 1833, a month after his death.[a]

Frederick Douglass: *Abolitionist, Orator, and Writer*

Frederick Douglass was born on a plantation in Talbot County, Maryland. The exact date of his birth is unknown, but he estimated that it was around February 1817. Douglass was born into slavery, was separated from his mother early in his life, and was sent to Baltimore to work. His master's wife taught him how to read, and from there Douglass began educating himself and teaching other slaves to read and write. In 1838, he escaped slavery and headed north. While in Massachusetts, he began to participate in abolitionist campaigns and became a member and preacher in the African Methodist Episcopal Zion Church. He went on to become an outstanding orator who fought the evil of slavery with passion that was formed and guided by Scripture. Douglass advised President Abraham Lincoln, and his work played a major role in the ratification of the Thirteenth Amendment in 1865.[b]

Catherine Booth: *Women's Advocate and Mother of the Salvation Army*

Catherine Booth was born in Ashourne, Derbyshire, England, in 1829. She was one of five children and was raised in a Christian home, where she learned Christian theology and read the entire Bible eight times by the age of twelve. Booth taught Sunday school and met her future husband, William Booth, after he preached a sermon she said was one of the best she'd ever heard. The couple had eight children and together founded the Salvation Army. Mrs. Booth advocated for exploited women and worked for the passage of the Criminal Law Amendment Act that contained general protections for women and raised the age of consent, passed in 1885.[c]

Dorothy Day: *Activist and Journalist*

Dorothy Day was born in Brooklyn, New York, in 1897. Early in life Day became interested in journalism, moved back to New York, and became a writer. She was active in antiwar and bohemian culture but eventually felt empty and lost in that lifestyle. In 1927, Dorothy and her daughter were baptized in a Roman Catholic Church, where she found new meaning and a biblical framework for redemptive social reform. Day co-founded the Catholic Workers Movement and the newspaper *The Catholic Worker*, and she dedicated her life to helping workers and the impoverished.[d]

Fannie Lou Hamer: *Advocate, Orator, and Organizer*
Fannie Lou Hamer was born in Montgomery County, Mississippi, in 1917. She was the youngest of twenty children, and her mother and father were sharecroppers. She was a devoted Baptist who believed that fighting for justice was her calling. In the 1960s, Hamer worked for the Student Nonviolent Coordinating Committee (SNCC) to demystify the political process for southern blacks and register them to vote—a dangerous endeavor in the Jim Crow South. Her faith in God was key to her ability to withstand police brutality, disenfranchisement, and involuntary sterilization (a "Mississippi appendectomy") while refusing to hate her oppressors. She was one of the most skilled orators and organizers in the civil rights movement and was known to have a powerful effect on audiences with her speeches and songs.[e]

Putting the Witness Before the Win

While politics can be used for good purposes, we shouldn't ignore the concerns of those who fear that it can corrupt individual Christians and taint the church. Throughout history Christians have certainly misused and been used by politics. We have supported unjust institutions and failed to correct elected officials who've harmed people.

Christians have to be deliberate about avoiding the pitfalls of political participation. While we certainly shouldn't plan to lose, Christians must keep in mind that we aren't engaging primarily to win political battles or to serve our own interest (1 Corinthians 10:24; Philippians 2:3-4). We already have the ultimate victory, which is our salvation and the kingdom that God has promised (Matthew 16:19; 25:34). Nothing in this world is comparable to our inheritance in the kingdom of God. No political ideology can replace the kingdom, nor does the kingdom of God rely on our political plans and priorities. Accordingly, we should participate in politics primarily to help others and to represent our Lord and Savior in the public square. This doesn't mean we have to ignore our own interests, but we can't be consumed and misled by them. Adherence to Jesus' teachings, such as the Sermon on the Mount, will prevent us from approaching politics in a self-serving way.

When in conflict we should demonstrate that our public witness is more important than winning a political battle. This means that if our side has to do something unloving or corrupt to win, then it's better for us to lose in that situation. We once heard a Christian political activist and donor express despair to a friend about the fact that his candidate lost in a presidential election. He told his friend that the lesson he learned from the loss was that "next time, we just can't tell the people what we actually want to do."

This is completely wrong. It's better to lose than to sacrifice our virtue for the sake of what is politically expedient, to defend leaders' harmful policies, or to condone immorality. It is better to lose that temporal battle. If our actions don't glorify God and serve as the salt and the light of the world, then they are good for nothing (Matthew 5:13-16).

The knock on many Christians in politics is that we use our religion as a cover to impose our prejudices and serve ourselves. Some of this criticism is unfair and malicious, but it has been true in too many instances. Just like Amaziah the priest in the book of Amos, some Christians have forsaken the Word of God for political favors and proximity to power (Amos 7:10-17). That's sinful because it undermines God's purpose for our own personal benefit.

Our primary purpose in life is to preach the gospel of Jesus Christ. That said, Christians should also participate in political activities because they give us a significant opportunity to actively love our neighbors by promoting their well-being and defending their best interests. The Bible and history show us that God's children can do great work in politics as long as they aren't *of* politics. There will be suffering and sin in the world until Jesus' return, but through the power of God we can make a difference and reflect the kingdom of God through the political sphere.

CHAPTER TWO

CHURCH

STATE

THE CIVIC PROCESS AND THE RELATIONSHIP
BETWEEN CHURCH AND STATE

The Bible is filled with kings, judges, pharaohs, governors, and procurators, all representing governments that often had a complicated relationship with the people of God. We see these dynamics in the Gospels when the religious leaders are politicking with Pontius Pilate to have Jesus crucified (John 18:28-40). The strife continues in the Epistles, where we're told about the suffering of the early church as they were being persecuted by Roman authorities (2 Corinthians 4:8-12; Hebrews 13:3). In contrast, in the Old Testament, King Cyrus of Persia made a "proclamation throughout his realm" ordering the reconstruction of the temple in Jerusalem and authorizing the Jews to go back home (Ezra 1:1-3). Scripture reveals a complex relationship between church and state.

Similarly, when we as Christians today engage the civic space, we're representatives of our Father in heaven. To properly go about our Father's business, we must be informed about the civic process and understand the relationship between church and state. What does the separation of church and state really mean? Are we supposed to invoke biblical principles when voting and advocating in the secular space among nonbelievers?

If we are to be effective citizens who steward our citizenship well, we must increase our civic literacy. Failing to understand the civic process and our relationship with government can result in a lot of wasted time and resources—or worse, we might hurt our cause, hurt others, or both. For instance, if we're concerned about public education and we picket our county board instead of our local school board (if there is one—this varies in different localities), then we're wasting our time. The same problem exists if we lobby our municipality about issues that are solely under federal purview, such as interstate commerce. Important causes and people in need lose precious political capital when their advocates are loud but don't clearly understand the process. This can make an important cause appear unworthy of consideration and leave vulnerable citizens without a fair hearing. It's like an unprepared attorney in a court case. The client suffers because of the attorney's incompetence. Taking the time to understand the mechanisms of government is basic due diligence that responsible citizens should feel an obligation to pursue.

The Purpose of Government

The apostle Paul says, "Let everyone be subject to the governing authorities, for there is no authority except that which God has established. The authorities that exist have been established by God" (Romans 13:1).

We serve a God of order. Genesis 1–2 shows us that God created an orderly world with rules, roles, and systems that are good. Some of God's creation was designed to be subdued and enjoyed while other things were to be left alone (Genesis 2:15-17). And ultimately, there were consequences for violating the guidelines God established (Genesis 3:17-19). Sin disrupted God's perfect order and made it impossible to recapture that perfection. Consequently, we swing between disorder and overly harsh rules, roles, and systems that trample on humanity's God-given rights.

Although church and state serve different functions, and although Christians are called to challenge state injustices when necessary, the fact remains that government is a God-ordained institution. Among other things, God uses government to bring a level of order to the world. Romans 13:4 states that the ruler "in authority is God's servant for your good. But if you do wrong, be afraid, for rulers do not bear the sword for no reason. They are God's servants, agents of wrath to bring punishment on the wrongdoer."

In their book *City of Man: Religion and Politics in a New Era*, Michael Gerson and Peter Wehner cite the works of Saint Augustine and American founding father John Jay to assert that order and safety are the first responsibilities of government. They go on to say, "Order is the sine qua non, the necessary precondition. Without it, we can hardly expect justice, prosperity, or virtue to flourish. And order cannot be achieved without government. It is an instrument sanctioned by God."[1]

Order is important because without it people are less likely to acknowledge their responsibilities, the rights of others, and human dignity in general. The strong have their way with the weak—without consequence—and human interactions are diminished by uncertainty and insecurity. Without consistent laws and systems, society can't create incentives for people to act justly, carefully, and nonviolently. The 2019 Global Peace Index found Afghanistan to be the most dangerous country in the world because of its political instability, number of deaths, number of internally displaced persons, corruption, and more.[2] In short, the country was missing the order that government was ordained to provide.

The United States judicial system makes sure that those who violate others are punished and that disputes are handled fairly and nonviolently. Ideally, citizens can expect to be held accountable if they infringe on the rights of others and recompensed if they're the victim of infringement or a breached agreement. A working justice system allows us to go about our daily lives with a level of certainty and security, which comes with a variety of positive societal effects. The aim of the judicial system is justice: treating people fairly and giving them what they deserve. Injustice is a form of disorder because it fails to respect the rights, property, and worth of others. What exactly justice entails and how far it should extend are constant subjects of political debate.

Since order, safety, and justice are the primary purposes of government, the best governments remain vigilant in guarding and promoting them. Yet no government gets it completely right. Some take order to the point of authoritarianism while others extend justice to allow people to impose their self-expression on others. Christians are called to comply with governing authorities (Romans 13:1); however, when a government ignores or supports injustice and disorder, Christians should not enable it or stand silently by (Proverbs 31:8-9; Isaiah 1:17). This will be discussed further in chapter seven.

Government Structure and Process

The United States has a democratic form of government, which means it derives its ultimate authority from the consent of its citizens who participate in this process through free and fair elections. As Abraham Lincoln stated in the Gettysburg Address, America is intended to be a "government of the people, by the people, for the people."[3] That said, it is important to understand that America is not a direct democracy, where people vote on every issue or provide their explicit approval for every governmental act. The US form of government is best described as a constitutional republic: citizens elect representatives to govern the country according to a framework established by the US Constitution.

The US Constitution instituted three branches of government for the federal system: legislative, executive, and judicial (see Branches of US Government figure). The legislative branch makes federal laws and is bicameral, which means it consists of two chambers: the House of Representatives and the Senate. The founding fathers created two congressional chambers to strike a balance between the interests of states of different sizes. States with larger populations get more members in the House of Representatives while every state gets two members in the Senate. In this system a state's population gives it a greater degree of influence without rendering smaller states completely powerless.

The House of Representatives contains 435 voting representatives from different states. Again, the number of representatives for each state is relative to its population. For instance, because California has the highest population, it has the most representatives at fifty-three. On the other hand, Alaska, Delaware,

Montana, North Dakota, South Dakota, Vermont, and Wyoming have just one representative each. Each representative has a two-year term.

The US Senate, sometimes referred to as "the greatest deliberative body in the world," has two members from each state for a total of one hundred members. Each member has a six-year term. Senators were initially chosen by state legislatures until the passage of the Seventeenth Amendment in 1913. Now the members of both chambers are voted on by the people in their respective states or congressional districts. The Senate provides the minority political party greater opportunity to influence its work than the House, and generally requires a greater deal of compromise and negotiation between the political parties in order to pass legislation. A law cannot move from the legislative branch to the executive branch until it has passed both the House of Representatives and the Senate.

The executive branch is responsible for executing and enforcing the laws created by the House of Representatives and the Senate. It consists of the president, vice president, cabinet, and executive agencies. The president is the head of the government and the commander in chief of the armed forces. The president selects the leaders of executive agencies, and together they work to implement the laws. When a law comes to the president from the legislative branch, the president either enacts the law by signing the legislation or vetoes the law. If the president vetoes the law, it goes back to the legislative branch, and both chambers must pass it by a two-thirds majority to override the presidential veto.

Last, the judicial branch, which includes the Supreme Court and other federal courts, interprets the laws. Judges who serve in the federal judiciary system are not elected directly by the people because the judicial branch is meant to be a nonpolitical body that applies the laws without being influenced by parties, popular opinion, or trends. These judges are appointed by the president and confirmed by the Senate. The nine justices on the Supreme Court all have lifetime appointments as do federal judges.

Each branch is designed to limit the authority of the other two branches so that none of them become too powerful. For instance, the president can't become a dictator because laws have to be passed by the legislative branch, which can remove the president by the process of impeachment. The judicial branch can review the president's actions and invalidate them if they're found to be unconstitutional. This is called the *separation of powers*, and it includes a system of checks and balances. Depending on the circumstances and a person's perspective, the

BRANCHES OF US GOVERNMENT

Constitution
Provides a separation of powers

LEGISLATIVE	EXECUTIVE	JUDICIAL
Creates laws	Carries out laws	Evaluates laws
CONGRESS	**THE ADMINISTRATION**	**COURT SYSTEM**
■ House of Representatives	■ President	■ Supreme Court
• 435 Members	• Commander in Chief	■ Federal Circuit Courts
• 2-year Terms	• 4-year Terms	■ Federal District Courts
■ Senate	• Head of State	
• 100 Members	■ Vice President	
• 6-year Terms	■ Cabinet	

separation of powers could either be blamed for making government action more difficult or praised as an ingenious arrangement that prevents the tyranny of the political whims and passions of the day.

The structure of state governments mostly mirrors that of the federal government. However, the authority of the federal government is limited by the power granted to the states. This is called *federalism*. This relationship is prescribed by the Tenth Amendment to the Constitution, ratified as part of the Bill of Rights in 1791, which states that "the powers not delegated to the United States by the Constitution, nor prohibited by it to the states, are reserved to the states respectively, or to the people."

States have their own constitutions and reserve the authority to create local and municipal governments. They elect their own leaders (governors, state representatives, and so on) and make decisions within state boundaries (regarding criminal justice, education, intrastate commerce, and so on) as long as these actions don't conflict with the US Constitution. The federal government can force states to abide by federal law when state laws or practices violate the US Constitution. For example, after the US Supreme Court passed the *Brown v. Board of Education of Topeka* decision in 1954, which made segregation in public education unlawful, the state of Alabama refused to desegregate its schools. After years of being pushed by activists, the federal government had to step in and force Alabama to abide by the federal law by sending the national guard to the state.

Political Parties

Political parties aren't mentioned in the Constitution, but they have become fundamental to our political system as vehicles for representation and a way to organize Americans who share some basic political commitments or views.

The two-party system in American politics is almost as old as the US government itself. Less than ten years after the signing of the Constitution, the first two political parties emerged: the Federalists and the Democrat-Republicans. Some of the founding fathers, including James Madison, were skeptical about the role parties would play, and some of those fears proved to be well-founded. Supporters of America's two-party system would contend that it's an imperfect way to add structure to elections and the political process, which would otherwise be even more chaotic and confusing. (We'll discuss parties further in chapter four.)

The Separation of Church and State

There's perhaps no constitutional concept that's more misunderstood than the separation of church and state. The phrase doesn't actually appear in the Constitution itself. In regard to the relationship between church and state, the First Amendment says, "Congress shall make no laws respecting an establishment of religion, or prohibiting the free exercise thereof." The first half of this provision is called the Establishment Clause, drafted to make sure the government wasn't promoting any particular religion. The Supreme Court established a three-part test to determine whether or not certain government actions constitute an "establishment of religion." The government can assist a religious institution if (1) the primary purpose of the assistance is secular, (2) the assistance neither promotes nor inhibits religion, and (3) there is no excessive entanglement between church and state.[4]

The second half of this provision is called the Free Exercise Clause. The Supreme Court interpreted the clause to mean that citizens have a right to practice their religion freely as long as the practice does not violate "public morals" or "compelling state interest."[5] In other words, the government can't penalize the church or churchgoers for their religious practices or beliefs without overcoming a very high test. Additionally, Title VII of the Civil Rights Act prohibits employers from discriminating against people based on their religion. Thus, an employer can't fire someone because of their religious practices or beliefs. These protections apply to people of all religions—not just Christianity.

Religious freedom is vital. God wants people to come to him freely, not out of government force or coercion. We should want the same. Religious freedom allows people of all faiths and none to act on their religious convictions without undue intrusion from the government. It offers protection from political retribution for religious groups that hold unpopular beliefs. Today in Egypt, Coptic Christians are killed for refusing to deny Christ. Americans don't experience that type of bloody persecution, but if we ignore the issue, religious institutions and individuals could be punished financially and professionally for abiding by religious principles. Christian colleges could be denied federal funding or be overexposed to expensive lawsuits and forced to close their doors.

We also know that the religious freedom of Christians is deeply tied to the religious freedom of those who are not Christian. The Religious Freedom Restoration Act (RFRA), one of the most important laws pertaining to religious freedom in our country, came about as a result of advocacy by a coalition of Americans from many different religious backgrounds. Since the law's passage in 1993, it has helped to protect the religious freedom of Native Americans, Sikhs, Jewish Americans, Muslims, Christians, and others. Because our constitution and our laws protect religious freedom, we can live our faith and share the gospel with others as part of a religious marketplace of ideas.

Many people have misinterpreted the separation of church and state to mean that religious views shouldn't play a role in public discussions and lawmaking. Someone might say, "We shouldn't restrict abortion because the pro-life perspective is based on religious values. It's a violation of the separation of church and state to impose those views on others." This is a gross misrepresentation of this constitutional principle. If that were the case, then stealing wouldn't be penalized because that too is based on a value judgment. Whether political views derive from religious tenets or secular philosophy, invoking values to influence the legislative process violates neither the constitution nor the spirit of the deliberative process.

This separation of church and state was not meant to prohibit religious values from influencing policies and the ways we build our common life together. It was meant to prohibit a relationship between the church and government like the founders were fleeing in England, where one denomination received a stamp of approval from the state as the official religion and others were persecuted or undermined. The separation of church and state prevents America from having a theocracy like Saudi Arabia or Sudan. It also prevents the government from using taxpayer dollars to directly fund evangelism efforts.

This is why many churches and religious bodies create separate 501(c)(3) nonprofit organizations for their institutional charitable work. This better facilitates public-private partnerships

—particularly financial partnerships—while keeping the lines between church and state clear for everyone involved. In a diverse and pluralistic society where not everyone agrees on what is right or shares the same faith, Christians should approach the public with a spirit of accommodation while holding firm to convictions.

As Christians, we should support the separation of church and state because we don't want the state infringing on our religious practices, and because we recognize the dangers of the church controlling the state. (Whose church would we choose?) We only wish to influence the state for the sake of human flourishing.

MARSH V. CHAMBERS (463 US 783)

Several United States Supreme Court cases have sought to define the relationship between government activity and religious affairs. In the 1983 landmark case *Marsh v. Chambers*, the Court decided that the Nebraska legislature's practice of opening sessions with prayer by a chaplain did not violate the Establishment Clause of the First Amendment. The chaplain, a Presbyterian minister who had served since 1965, was paid with public funds.

The Court reasoned that the tradition of opening legislative sessions with prayer is deeply embedded in this country's history. Indeed, the tradition had been practiced during the Colonial Era and has existed in Nebraska for over one hundred years. Similarly, the practice of paying chaplains with public funds has deep historic roots tracing back to the First Congress. Therefore, the drafters of the First Amendment clearly thought the practice of legislative prayer was consistent with the Establishment Clause of the First Amendment.

The Court also noted that the chaplain's prayer neither disparaged other faiths nor sought to advance a particular faith.

Thus, the fact that the chaplain was long-serving and from only one denomination was not enough, by itself, to violate the First Amendment. *Marsh v. Chambers* is noteworthy for its recognition that "we are a religious people whose institutions presuppose a Supreme Being." Therefore, seeking divine guidance on public bodies through prayer does not offend the Constitution but serves to acknowledge our widely held religious beliefs.[a]

Law and Values

The separation of church and state was not intended to prevent Christians or any other religious group from promoting or applying their values in the policymaking process. All citizens have the right to advocate and vote based on their values, whether secular or religious. In fact, all policies and laws come from some set of values. It's impossible to create a law without making a decision about what is right and wrong or what is beneficial and harmful. Each decision is based on the particular values being applied to the issue at hand.

A person's values are principles and standards of behavior, and laws are correspondingly based on principles and standards of behavior. The idea that it's possible to separate the values of the people from their laws is absurd. As Americans, we protect life, liberty, and the pursuit of happiness because those are things we find to be of great worth. We tend to assume that certain fundamental American values are obvious and accepted by humanity generally, but this is not the case. Indeed, even what is considered to be an American value has changed over the course of our history, and defining what is and is not an American value is often at the very heart of our political discourse. Predominant values in nations or regions of the world affect the political conversation and public policy in a range of areas. This is, perhaps, most obvious when it comes to areas such as immigration policy, economic policy, and human rights, but there are countless ways values are reflected in even the most seemingly mundane policy areas, such as traffic laws or zoning regulations.

Value judgments are an inescapable aspect of political engagement and decision making. If we're not applying our values to our advocacy and voting, then we're applying someone else's. Christians who support "abortion on demand" aren't being neutral; their position is motivated by values just like anyone else's, be they values aligned with libertarianism or utilitarianism or nihilism. A Christian juror who tries to give someone a harsher sentence because of their race is applying supremacist beliefs instead of a Christian ethic (Deuteronomy 16:19-20, John 7:24). Engaging the political arena invariably involves making value judgments. Where we search for those answers exposes where our faith resides.

As Christians, failing to apply biblical values to our political decisions is unfaithful to our mission. Christianity is not just about going to church. It's a way of seeing and understanding the world around us that should affect everything we do. In other words, Christianity is both a lifestyle and a worldview. We can't separate what we believe in the political arena from who we are in Christ and what obedience to God demands (1 Samuel 15:22). Jesus told Christians to "love the Lord your God with all your heart and with all your soul and with all your mind" (Matthew 22:37). This is the greatest of Jesus' commandments, and it doesn't leave any room for us to disregard his guidelines in politics or any other aspect of life. Our adherence to progressivism or conservatism must be subordinated to the guidelines of the Word.

That said, not every tenet of Christianity should become the law of the state. We're not called to create a government that simply enforces our religion. Christianity is not about coercing people into agreeing with us. When the faith has been misrepresented that way in the past, it has caused great atrocities. We see this in the excesses of the Christian Crusades, when many nonbelievers were killed at the direction of religious leaders. A religion with a history of being persecuted should know better than to become the persecutor.

When confronted with a political question, we should consult Scripture, church tradition, and social teaching to glean wisdom and direction. This book will discuss a range of principles and values derived from Scripture that can influence how to think about politics. Certainly Scripture is replete with special consideration for the "disinherited," to use Howard Thurman's word, or as Catholic social teaching offers, a "preferential option for the poor."[6] Scripture teaches that human beings are made in the image of God, and we believe that understanding should be respected in our laws and society. The Christian tradition offers a deep concern for the person and for personhood: people are not to be treated as tools or mere economic units but as whole human beings who are meant to thrive and flourish. We must affirm human dignity.

These ideas have influenced political thinking around the world. The idea that Christianity has something to offer in the realm of government and public policy is not unique to modern America. Accordingly, there is great diversity in Christian political thought. Some ideas, such as justifications for chattel slavery, are categorically wrong regardless of the context. Other political ideas are appropriate for a particular time, place, and society, but not for another. Faithfulness does not demand support for any one economic theory or form of government, and Christians should consider the culture and structures of their society as they are applying their values.

For instance, in a pluralistic, democratic society, it is wise in our judgment for Christians to be able to articulate the practical impact of biblical values and how they benefit people and society generally. This does not mean we can never cite Scripture or speak definitively from our own point of view, but it does mean that we should always have an eye toward what is edifying for our neighbors and what will most help them. For instance, if we want further regulations on pornography, we need to be able to explain its negative impacts on society from a common-good perspective rather than simply pointing to what Scripture says about lust and adultery of the heart. We can point to the dangers of pornography's accessibility to children, higher rates of assault linked to pornography use, and pornography's role in divorce rates.[7]

Furthermore, Christians should be able to respect and work constructively with nonbelievers in the public square. Law professor John Inazu has written about what he calls "confident pluralism," which he explains this way:

> The civic practices of confident pluralism build upon three aspirations: *tolerance*, *humility* and *patience*. . . . It might seem less obvious that we would pursue tolerance, humility, and patience in light of our firmly held convictions. But it is in fact the confidence in our own views in the midst of deep difference that allows us to engage charitably with others. Rather than lashing out at others or remaining in our own echo chambers, we can pursue dialogue and coexistence even when (and perhaps especially when) we believe that our views are in fact the better ones.[8]

As Christians, we can engage with others kindly and respectfully when we're confident about what we believe. In Acts 17, we see the apostle Paul demonstrate this in Athens as he interacts with other thinkers in the agora, which was the marketplace of ideas (Acts 17:16-32). He wasn't trying to coerce people; he was trying to relate to and persuade them.

Conclusion

The structure and operation of the American government are controlled by the US Constitution. To engage politics effectively, Christians should be familiar with primary constitutional principles and the relationship between the state and the church. While many people wrongly believe that the separation of church and state excludes religious values from influencing policymaking, that couldn't be further from the truth. Church and state are separate insofar as the state should never establish a religion or infringe on the free practice thereof. Still, church and state are not isolated from one another. Each always influences and affects the other. The government should be directed by the principles and interests of the people, religious and secular alike.

It's impossible to separate the values of the people from their laws. Laws are always an application of some group's values. Ideally, everyone would agree on what these values should be—and sometimes everyone does. But when that isn't possible, we must promote our values within the legislative process. We can do this with respect for those who disagree, understanding that not every precept in the Bible is meant to be a law of the state. We do this by orienting our politics toward a vision of what is truly good for all the people, even those who hold very different beliefs or interests. This is what it means to love our neighbors in politics.

CHAPTER THREE

COMPASSION

CONVICTION

CIVIC ENGAGEMENT THROUGH
A BIBLICAL FRAMEWORK

N o one makes political decisions from a neutral position. To make a policy decision is to choose certain values and goods over others. Political decisions are inevitably informed by a certain worldview or outlook. When Christians aren't applying biblical principles to their political opinions, their point of view is guided by other belief systems.

The gospel of Jesus Christ is the ultimate authority in all arenas of life, including politics. This means the gospel should be the foundation and starting point of our political decisions. Our preferences, interests, and sociopolitical ideologies aren't the ultimate authority and can't take precedence over biblical principles. Outside ideologies and philosophies can inform us, but they should never be the masters of our political action.

The Bible does not provide a political platform, and we should be careful to not confuse our personal policy preferences with religious doctrine. Two Christians can disagree on an important policy without one or the other necessarily being unfaithful. For instance, the Bible doesn't tell us exactly how much in taxes government should collect or what the minimum wage should be. Even when the Bible does directly speak to an issue, Christians might disagree on how to apply the principle in the public square. It's a mistake to suggest that Christians should always come to the same political conclusions. However, all Christians should make those decisions from a biblical framework.

Frameworks provide us with room to disagree while creating clear boundaries delineating what is inside and outside of our value system. They allow a level of flexibility to consider different preferences and interests. Based on our life experiences, geographic region, or profession, we might honestly come to different conclusions on policy within the same general framework. That said, some positions are clearly outside what's prescribed by the Bible. Christians clearly should not support solutions that undermine human dignity by, for example, unfairly discriminating, creating excessive criminal punishments, eroding religious liberty, undervaluing the lives of the unborn, and so on.

As Christians, we must be deliberate about making sure our positions have biblical roots rather than being controlled by our political party or ideological tribe. In Colossians 2:8, the apostle Paul exhorts, "See to it that no one takes you captive through hollow and deceptive philosophy, which depends on human tradition and elemental spiritual forces of this world rather than on Christ." We run into trouble when worldly perspectives control our moral outlook and override our Christian principles. Our political opinions must be based on biblical standards and not dependent on human ideas. We must assess the issues within a framework that emphasizes love and truth, compassion and conviction, social justice and moral order. Our political decisions must demonstrate love for our neighbors while observing the timeless truths God has revealed to us through Scripture.

There is no single Christian policy or political plan. To act like there is one, or to wish that there was one, would be to make the old mistake of thinking that the kingdom of God is like human kingdoms. The goal is not to have all Christians share the same exact politics but to have all Christians think *Christianly* about politics. Thinking about politics from a biblical framework doesn't mean we'll always agree, but it does exclude some policies and forms of advocacy that are counter to our beliefs.

Politics is a limited but essential forum for pursuing the well-being of our neighbors. It is limited in both its scope and its effectiveness. Politics can and should only reach so much and so far because political solutions will never approach the perfect justice that Jesus brings. Our hope in all things is in him.

This chapter sets out a biblical framework for engaging political questions with biblical fidelity and confidence.

A False Choice

Do you advocate social justice or family values? Do you support women or are you against abortion? Do you love the poor or do you believe in personal responsibility?

Don't answer those questions—or at least not in the way they're asked. They are based on a false premise and thus create a false dilemma for Christians. This is what happens when we allow the world to frame the questions and the issues for us: we end up choosing one of two wrong answers or rejecting one of two right answers, and losing control of our public witness in the process. Part of getting the correct answer is about framing the issues correctly.

When Christians enter the political arena, we often feel like we're forced to choose between two very flawed options that compromise our beliefs. This is because the US political system is dangerously polarized and both sides frame the issues to fit incomplete or dishonest narratives. As you can see, when the issue isn't framed properly, there often isn't a correct answer.

America's current political system separates love from truth, compassion from conviction, and social justice from moral order as if they're somehow at odds with one another. People who support social justice issues generally don't support traditional views of morality and vice versa. But there's no clear reason why those two stances should be separate. It's just presented to us as the only way, and we accept it. Most people aren't aware that a viable alternative exists.

Here's how these competing narratives usually play out: those on the right side of the political spectrum say they stand for individual freedom, patriotism, and moral order; the left, on the other hand, claims to stand for justice, equality, and inclusion. Conservatives say progressives are immoral because of their positions on abortion, religious liberty, and the like. Progressives say conservatives are bigoted and lack compassion when it comes to poverty, race, and gender. Both sides have become less tolerant of differing viewpoints and often stamp out candidates and advocates who hold a more nuanced or moderate perspective.

Many Christians are conflicted because they believe in freedom, moral order, justice, equality, and inclusion. We want to protect the unborn *and* treat the poor and racial minorities with love and compassion. We also see merit in the criticisms of each side. Yet because of how the issues are presented, Christians are told to either surrender their biblical convictions or neglect their Christlike compassion.

There's nothing wrong with being conflicted about how both options are right in part and wrong in part. The bigger problem is when Christians are unaware or unbothered by the faults on the side they prefer. This isn't to suggest a false equivalency between the two parties. One party might be more wrong on more issues at a given time, but we must realize that both fall well short of the biblical standard.

Christians can choose a political party, but we can't choose between love and truth. We can't fully embrace movements that dismiss justice or undermine moral order. Fannie Lou Hamer and Dorothy Day didn't buy into these distorted categories. Their civic engagement spoke to the importance of both social justice and moral order, and they were confident enough to do so without apology.

Christians must be critical thinkers and question the assumptions and conclusions presented to us. We shouldn't simply accept the issues as they've been framed by political parties, ideological tribes, or the media—because these sources usually aren't analyzing the issues from the standard of the gospel. Instead, these groups often frame the issue in a way that leads us to the conclusions they desire. But Christians must make sure biblical doctrine is the framework from which we base our answers to political and cultural questions. Once we frame an issue properly, we're able not only to respond in a more accurate and faithful manner but also to disarm the false choices that can entangle us.

Instead of answering the questions at the beginning of this section as they were posed, Christians should say, "I support social justice, morality, and family values. I don't affirm ungodly behavior, nor do I hate the individual; I affirm the human dignity of all people. I love and care for the poor, and I believe in personal responsibility." In other words, proper framing allows us to embrace the love and truth of the gospel. Christians can reject false choices in politics without walking away from civic engagement altogether.

The Framework: Social Justice and Moral Order

Thankfully, the Bible provides us with a clear framework for engaging our neighbors, which generally applies to politics and culture. The essence of the framework is mentioned by the apostle Paul in Ephesians 4.

Paul was writing to the church of Ephesus, which was known as "the persevering church" (see Revelation 2:1-3). They had endured a lot of suffering and had false prophets who were trying to infiltrate the church with false teachings. Without the proper framework for addressing their issues, the Ephesians were at risk of being misguided into unbiblical doctrine and actions. In analyzing this situation, Paul informs the church that mature believers are not easily influenced or deceived like children. In Ephesians 4:14, he says, "then we will no longer be infants, tossed back and forth by the waves, and blown here and there by every wind of teaching and by the cunning and craftiness of people in their deceitful scheming." In other words, mature Christians are not swayed by false teachers because they have a strong relationship with God and know what they believe. They are able to apply the proper framework regardless of what popular culture, academia, or political leaders are saying. But what exactly is this framework?

41

In the next verse Paul says that mature believers are able to speak "the truth in love." This might seem like a simple assertion, but it's enormously significant. Paul is saying that in all situations, Christians must be truthful and loving at the same time. Through days of abundance, famine, or persecution, followers of Christ speak the truth in love because our beliefs aren't determined by our circumstances. Jesus himself was "full of grace and truth" (John 1:14), just as the gospel requires us to be committed to both loving others—showing them grace and compassion—and standing up for biblical convictions and the truth of God's Word. Paul's prophetic words dismantle the false choice and reveal the error in thinking we must choose one or the other. These instructions have relevance for our lives today, including how to think about politics. Christians ought to evaluate all political issues through the love and truth of the gospel. This is a *both-and* proposition, not *either-or*. The world separates the two, but the gospel transcends the false divide and shows that we must value both.

Love and Justice

Let's take a look at the love component of this gospel-centered framework. The gospel is saturated with a love imperative. Statements about the importance of love are woven through the Bible. Jesus even gave us a "new commandment" when he said, "Love one another. As I have loved you, so must you love one another" (John 13:34). In the Synoptic Gospels he adds, "Love your neighbor as yourself" (Mark 12:31).

It's impossible to read the Gospels without encountering Jesus' emphasis on love. From Nicodemus and the woman at the well to the thief beside him on the cross, Jesus broke with tradition to extend kindness and mercy to sinners and saints alike (John 3:1 21; 4:4 42; Luke 23:32-43). He also taught us to care for the poor and fellowship with them as he revealed their great worth (Mark 12:41-44; Luke 14:12-14). This love imperative isn't based on the social status of who we're interacting with or what environment we're in. Accordingly, it also extends to our engagement in the public square. Christian advocacy and political positions must reflect the love and compassion of Jesus Christ.

This means we must seek justice for our neighbors. Justice is about the right ordering of things, and we look to Scripture to help us determine what that might look like. We know Jesus will eventually set all wrongs right, but until then he has invited us to join him in his work. Politics is an essential arena for pursuing justice. The political sphere provides us with a significant opportunity to actively love our neighbors by acknowledging their dignity and seeking their well-being through the civic process. Love for others should compel us to advocate for justice on their behalf just as we would do for ourselves. When we're confronted with a societal problem we must consider the best solution out of love, compassion, and justice. This will cause us to defend the poor, the immigrant, and the widow, and to treat those who have committed criminal offenses with fairness. As we assess policies, we should pay special attention to how they will affect people, particularly those who are less fortunate, rather than treating public policy as a way to advance ideas without any regard for their practical impact. We should not support policy or rhetoric that demeans any group, nor view our convictions or our political power as justification for bullying any group or any person. Love and justice can never be absent from our public witness.

Truth and Moral Order

Jesus said, "If you hold to my teaching, you are really my disciples. Then you will know the truth, and the truth will set you free" (John 8:31-32).

A pilot who flies southeast to reach a destination north of his original location is misguided. He'll never reach his intended destination unless he corrects his course. Similarly, in politics and culture, people often go in the wrong direction to reach their objective—or even have the wrong destination altogether. As Christians, part of our purpose is to direct people toward the love of Christ, which acknowledges the dignity of all people, and toward his truth, which allows for human flourishing.

Jesus came into the world to bear witness to the truth; he's our North Star (John 14:6; 18:37). Accordingly, as Christians our mission is to follow his example and spread his truth no matter the cost (Matthew 28:16-20; 2 Corinthians 4:2). This mission extends into our political engagement, which must always be founded on God's truth.

The Bible is the absolute standard for truth and moral order (Psalm 119:160; John 14:6; 2 Timothy 3:16-17). What it says is good is good. What it says is righteous is righteous. All other statements of truth must be judged based on the biblical standard. Scripture reveals God's design and provides us with structure, guidance, and purpose. Without it, life is meaningless and directionless. We can't identify right and wrong or find the correct solutions without first acknowledging the truth. The pilot from the previous example might truly believe southeast is north—but that doesn't make it true and it won't get him any closer to his proper destination. Until he recognizes true north, he's hopelessly lost.

The Bible often uses light as a metaphor for truth, describing disobedience and distance from God as darkness (Psalm 43:3; 119:105; John 8:12). As Christians, we are the light of the world, and in order to lead people in the right direction we must base our opinions and actions on what is true, not merely on our preferences or feelings (Matthew 5:14). We can't defer to popular opinion or lean on our own understanding when it comes to moral issues (Proverbs 3:5-6).

Christian advocacy and policy positions must be informed by the truth of the gospel. But there is rarely only one Christian position on a public policy issue. We don't want to prescribe specific policy approaches as the only faithful application of gospel truth. All political systems are imperfect, as are the people in them. However, we must think Christianly as we take political action. Ignoring God's guidelines cannot lead us to just outcomes. Among other things, the moral order God established in Scripture warns against shedding innocent blood, bearing false witness, or pursuing sexual relationships outside of marriage between one man and one woman. We hurt ourselves and others when our politics deny this moral order. God's ways are not our ways, and we deceive ourselves when we think we know better than God (Isaiah 55:8-9).

The world tells us that our values should evolve with the times and suggests that every individual has their own truth. This might sound pleasant, but it simply isn't a biblical understanding of truth. What God revealed in Genesis and what Jesus taught millennia ago is just as true and relevant today. Times change, but God is unchanging and his Word is everlasting (Psalm 119:89; Isaiah 40:8; 1 Peter 1:25). Whether our pilot flies in the year 1950 or 2020, southeast isn't north and never will be, regardless of his opinion. Our own personal truth can't liberate us; only God's truth sets us free (John 8:31-32; 1 John 1:6).

It is possible, and perhaps inescapable, for public policy to either promote or undermine moral order. For instance, the Bible is clear about the relationships and obligations between a husband and wife, and between parents and their children. Economic policies that disincentivize marriage and make it economically advantageous to divorce or not get married in the first place, often referred to as a "marriage penalty," fail to uphold moral order. A criminal justice system that unnecessarily separates parents from their children through overincarceration fails to apply an understanding of the family unit as a reflection of moral order. Public policies that treat marriage and the unique and natural bond between a mother, a father, and their child as irrelevant distort moral order.

The law is a teacher. When the law teaches the wrong lessons, it is our responsibility to listen and follow the teachings of Jesus and not allow politics to determine our values. However the societal effect of law is undeniable. If the law teaches that human life is disposable, that will corrode the nation's moral infrastructure. If the law teaches that sexual freedom is an ultimate end, that will corrode the nation's moral infrastructure. If the law teaches that economic profit is society's chief aim, that will corrode the nation's moral infrastructure.

How to apply moral standards to politics can be complicated. Multiple moral truths might be in conflict when considering a single political decision. Policies that would seem to advance a moral truth might end up undermining it. Indeed, sometimes it is wise to accept that the best use of the law in a given situation is not to enforce morality but rather to allow for the freedom to be moral. The important thing is that we do not pretend or delude ourselves into thinking that politics is not a moral enterprise. Christians must consider what they know to be true and good in politics, as they do in other aspects of their lives.

Indeed, we should be careful to ensure that we do not invoke moral order only in regard to issues that don't affect us directly. Christians should be sure that they first apply any standard to themselves and those ideas most personal to them before thinking about how that standard affects others (Matthew 7:5). No-fault divorce laws were passed nearly twenty years before the first statewide same-sex marriage referendum. Some Christians protest the building of a mosque in their town when there have been strip clubs and casinos there for years. Is this because Christians can imagine themselves getting divorced or wanting to visit a strip club but believe that same-sex marriage and religious freedom for Muslims are issues that only concern other people? God's moral order speaks to issues of greed, corruption, manipulation, and violence as well. Be certain that you're not more eager to invoke God's moral order for others than you are for yourself.

Truth is not subject to popular opinion. There was a time when the majority of American society thought black people were inherently inferior. Notwithstanding the majority's opinion, that assertion was false. If more people had interpreted the Bible with clean hearts and clear eyes, they would never have indulged in that deception. We shouldn't be persuaded by whatever side of the argument has greater numbers.

As Christians we should always be learning and identifying societal issues that need to be fixed for the sake of our neighbors. We mustn't forget, however, that truth is established by the Bible; it must frame our civic engagement.

Love and Truth

The world struggles to maintain love and truth simultaneously. Through the gospel, however, Christians can both love their neighbors and bear witness to timeless truth without contradiction. Love and truth are not mutually exclusive. In fact, it's just the opposite: love and truth are interdependent. Pastor Tim Keller once said that "love without truth is sentimentality (overly emotional and lacking substance) and truth without love is harshness."[1] We can know the Bible front to back and be adept in our understanding of systematic theology, but if we don't love our neighbors, we're not being Christlike. If we use doctrine to correct people but don't show them love and compassion, not only will we be ineffective but more importantly we'll fail to follow Christ's example. The apostle Paul says, "If I have the gift of prophecy and can fathom all mysteries and all knowledge, and if I have faith that can move mountains, but do not have love, I am nothing" (1 Corinthians 13:2). He also says, "clothe yourselves with compassion, kindness, humility, gentleness and patience" (Colossians 3:12).

A ministry that's focused on doctrine but lacks love is actually lacking truth too. When we address people harshly and lack grace, we're likely to overlook the whole of their situation and ignore our own faults. Consequently, we only deal with part of the truth and become hypocritical. In order to be completely truthful, we must be conscious of our own faults and extend grace to others just as God extends grace to us. This applies to how we engage civically too. Our ability to evangelize and promote morality is encumbered if we don't go out of our way to make sure people are treated fairly in the public square. For example, you can't credibly promote family values if you're not concerned about fathers being taken out of their homes for extended periods due to unjust prison sentences.

Similarly, we can't be loving in a biblical sense without acknowledging truth. The world often understands love as a formless feeling of affirmation, niceness, or even lust. But the biblical definition of love is much more powerful and fulfilling. Love is about willing the good for another. It's about support, self-sacrifice, and compassion. We love because God first loved us, and that love is undergirded by truth. Love that is unwilling to be truthful with others is empty and shortsighted. God disciplines those he loves, and the best discipline is aimed at obedience to truth and right behavior (Proverbs 3:12).

If our social justice advocacy isn't rooted in doctrine and truth, then we'll end up promoting things contrary to biblical teachings. This can be applied to many political issues and movements. Take the issue of gambling, for example. While gambling is not expressly forbidden in Scripture, it tends to cultivate opportunities for vices like greed and materialism. In many localities, government has not just taken an indifferent view toward gambling but has encouraged it by providing incentives for the establishment of gambling operations. Many states have a state lottery, which essentially operates as a kind of regressive, voluntary tax on the poor and working class. Politicians and voters rationalize this by directing the funds gained by lottery fees to something such as public education—but is that justification or obfuscation? Christians have the ability to act in politics for a vision of what our communities should and could be. There might be multiple Christian views on an issue like gambling or state lotteries, but each of those views should involve contending with doctrine and the teachings of Scripture. "We live in a modern age" or "everyone is doing it" are not sufficient explanations.

Since the gospel of Jesus Christ is both love and truth, Christians should recognize the imbalance and incompleteness present when one of them is missing. Engaging the public square within a biblical framework involves promoting love and truth, social justice and moral order. Accordingly, a public witness that rejects either love or truth is not faithful.

The Flaws in Our Political Ideologies

Christians are usually proficient at identifying the flaws on the other side of the political spectrum and pointing out how our political opponents fall short of the gospel. But we're less willing or able to identify the issues on our own end of the spectrum. Neither progressivism nor conservatism satisfies the love or truth imperatives of the gospel. Both fall outside of a biblical framework. Christians must recognize the failings and blind spots in their own political party and ideological tribe in order to avoid indoctrination and to faithfully correct unexamined assumptions.

At certain times and on certain issues Christian principles compel us to defy both political conservatism and political progressivism. When it comes to political ideology, to be conservative or progressive at all times and on every issue is not only to be intellectually lazy and easily manipulated, but also it's unfaithful. Theological conservatism and ideological conservatism aren't always the same. The far left's conception of social justice isn't always consistent with the biblical understanding.

In urban and academic settings most people pride themselves on being progressive. Progressivism often focuses on changing systems and institutions, and challenging old assumptions that hurt marginalized groups such as racial minorities, women, and the poor. Cultural progressives seek to remove traditional constraints and stigmas for a more free and open society. During the Progressive Era (1890s–1920s), reformers like Upton Sinclair exposed how industrialization and political corruption harmed Americans, and he focused on reforming labor laws, safety standards, anticorruption law, and the like.[2] These reforms saved many lives and improved quality-of-life standards.

However, progressivism often falls short of the truth and the moral order presented in the gospel. When we think about what it means to be progressive, we think about moving forward and fixing things. That can be good, but being progressive is not the solution to every situation. For instance, if you're on the edge of a cliff, to progress or lean forward isn't such a good idea. Moving forward is a bad idea if you're already headed in the wrong direction (think of the pilot). Sometimes God is asking us to stand firm on his Word or to preserve ideas and institutions that he's already established as good. Modern thought tells us that we can improve everything—but God's truth can't be improved.

Another downside of progressivism is that it can incorrectly assume that traditions and old mores are negative and that they erode systems and institutions indiscriminately. Changing bad institutions like Jim Crow and mass incarceration of black and brown males is good, but not all institutions are bad and need to be disrupted. Institutions like the church and the family should not be eroded to advance ideological ends. When it comes to abortion and the Christian family and sexual ethics, progressivism tries to place an expiration date that doesn't exist on truth. A Christian who follows progressivism uncritically will end up denying biblical doctrine at some point to keep up with this ever-evolving ideology. When a Christians allow progressive ideology to diminish the role of Scripture and deny the timelessness of truth, we trade solid ground for sinking sand (Matthew 7:24-27).

Conservatism, on the other hand, often focuses on preserving social order and maximizing individual and economic freedom by limiting the role of government. The conservative icon Ronald Reagan said there were three legs of conservatism: national security, economic conservatism, and social conservatism. Generally, conservatism acknowledges that the state is not capable of fulfilling the role of the family or mediating institutions. At most, government exists to supplement and protect those institutions, not to replace them. Some would say conservatism is also more realistic about human nature and the reality of limited resources. In some instances social conservatism has warded off corrosive menaces like pornography and euthanasia. It has also emphasized the importance of work and personal responsibility, which are biblical values (Proverbs 12:11; 1 Timothy 5:8).

The downside of conservatism is that it often fails to show love and show justice—vital components of a gospel-centered framework. Conservatism can assume an equal playing field that doesn't exist between different demographics, and it can be so focused on principles and systems—such as unfettered markets and an antagonism toward the federal government—that it overlooks how people are actually doing under those systems and principles. Historically, many conservatives have failed to adequately acknowledge and correct past racial injustice. For example, leaders of the conservative movement such as William Buckley failed to support the civil rights movement, often antagonizing it instead. As conservative thinker Jonah Goldberg admitted in 2002, "Conservatives—though not Republicans—were often at best MIA on the issue of civil rights in the 1960s. Liberals were on the right side of history on the issue of race. And conservatives should probably admit that more often."[3] Furthermore, efforts like the Moral Majority that promoted "family values" were uncompassionate toward those they deemed immoral. Such callousness distorts Christianity because it lacks the grace of Jesus Christ and makes Christians appear more judgmental than merciful. Today, many social conservatives still don't support the kind of social justice Scripture esteems.

Thus, a Christian who views politics primarily through a conservative rather than Christian lens might underemphasize love and compassion and deal with others harshly.

When the Bible Is Silent

The Bible doesn't speak to every political issue. We might have political preferences that the Bible neither affirms nor forbids. We need to be honest about that and not use the Bible to fortify a position that faithful Christians can see differently. For instance, the Bible doesn't tell us exactly what economic system we must use, even though Christians often try to use the Bible to support a specific economic system. Different economic systems might come with different problems, but pretending that God has ordained a particular preference oversteps the bounds of Scripture.

We also have to be wise and discerning about our particular place, time, and context. We might make a rule for our personal life, our family, or our church, but that does not necessarily make it wise to instill that same rule as public policy, particularly in a diverse society. In all cases, Christians should pursue the good of their neighbors and be able to advance their political preferences as such.

Christians can disagree on policy. We've provided a simple framework that allows for disagreement. Christians won't always come to the same conclusions on every issue, but this framework gives us a lot of common ground on political matters closely tied to the love and truth of the gospel.

Conclusion

The public square is full of ideas, theories, and philosophies about what to value and how to make the world better, and these things can be helpful or harmful. If we don't think about them through the lens of the gospel, we'll be prone to be led away from what is good and true. Biblical doctrine must be the foundation of our civic involvement. We must be led by love and truth as we think critically about political issues and search for solutions.

Our identity shouldn't be tied up in either progressivism or conservatism. We shouldn't hesitate to correct either when necessary. When conservatism means preserving unjust systems and institutions, it must be opposed. When progressivism means moving from God's truth, it too must be opposed.

CHAPTER FOUR

PARTNERSHIPS

PARTISANSHIP

COBELLIGERENCE AND CRITICAL THINKING

B efore large companies enter into partnerships, they often negotiate with their potential partner for months. Their attorneys go back and forth to make sure the other party is who they claim to be and that their client's reputation and assets will be protected. The parties sign complicated contracts that are hundreds of pages long, and after coming to an agreement the arrangement is audited from time to time to ensure continuing compliance. And even so, the courts are still full of lawsuits from partnerships gone wrong. People or whole organizations fail to uphold their end of the bargain, and unforeseen events hasten the failure of once promising joint ventures.

The church's political and cultural partnerships might not have the same technical jargon, but they are often just as complicated and the stakes are just as high—if not higher. The public square can be a tricky and even treacherous place. Ulterior motives often hide behind benevolent causes, and it can be difficult to discern the true character of others until it's too late.

The church's reputation can be damaged by negligently teaming up with bad actors. For instance, Billy Graham infamously allied with Richard Nixon's presidential campaign—and came to regret it.[1] At one point Nixon opportunistically had Graham deliver political messages that Nixon knew to be deceptive.[2] Nixon would later have to resign the presidency after the Watergate scandal, leaving the reputation of "America's Pastor" marred in the process.

Unfortunately, Christians rarely go through an arduous due-diligence process in evaluating cultural and political partners before joining forces. Many Christians rush into such relationships while others avoid partnering with nonbelievers altogether. But history proves that Christians can work with nonbelievers to pursue God's will and improve the lives of their neighbors. For example, Ezra and Nehemiah worked with Persian authorities to rebuild the temple and the wall in Jerusalem (Ezra 1:1–7:28; Nehemiah 1:1–7:3). Christian activists have also successfully worked with nonbelievers to fight injustices in America. Jesus called us to be the salt and the light of the world (Matthew 5:13-16). Christians can't fully pursue that commission if they're not in contact with people outside of the faith and willing to assist those pursuing positive goals even if their foundation isn't biblical.

The structure of the US political system and the diversity of our society make it difficult to accomplish political tasks without working with people outside a Christian belief system. The fast pace of society means we aren't always able to negotiate for very long, but there are steps Christians can take to prevent walking into traps and damaging our Christian witness through our political partnerships. This chapter discusses how to enter into partnerships with nonbelievers and even learn from them without taking on their identity or bowing to their idols. It details why our partnerships must always be strategic and conditional, and why our interactions must be honest yet shrewd.

Partnerships

There are many different types of partnerships. Some involve formal agreements with legal entities while others are more informal. Some are ad hoc (for a particular purpose) while others are long term and based on more general interests. For the purposes of this book, a *partnership* is two or more people purposefully working together in pursuit of a common cultural, political, or economic cause. The ancient Greek philosopher Aristotle said that every political partnership aims at "some good," meaning the purpose of a political partnership is to achieve a joint objective valued by the group.[3]

When it comes to politics, there's power in numbers. In a representative democracy, bringing about change or maintaining things you value means galvanizing and persuading a significant number of people to support your issue. Partnerships are an essential part of this process. For example, labor unions were created because workers realized that they had more leverage to change work conditions and pay when they worked together rather than individually. It is incredibly difficult, if not impossible, to provoke significant political change in a diverse society like the United States without forming partnerships.

Partnerships can be beneficial because they create opportunities for shared resources, experience, expertise, and comradery. Strategic and resourceful citizens form coalitions that shore up their weaknesses and complement their strengths. Partners learn skills from one another and exchange insights.

But partnerships can also be difficult. Even when people come together with a common goal, their interests might not be completely aligned or might only align temporarily. They may hold different values or have conflicting outside interests. A partner today could be a political opponent tomorrow. Many Christians are hesitant to enter into partnerships with nonbelievers because the ultimate goal of Christians, to serve and glorify God, isn't shared by nonbelievers. Many also fear that the work will be tainted by ungodly motivations. These legitimate concerns are addressed in-depth later in this chapter.

However, the truth is that completely avoiding partnerships and interactions with nonbelievers is virtually impossible. As Aristotle pointed out, the city-state itself is a partnership; you're already in a partnership with nonbelievers just by virtue of being an American citizen. We've all implicitly agreed to what philosophers such as Thomas Hobbes and John Locke referred to as the social contract: as citizens, we've jointly agreed to give up certain things (such as money through taxes) in exchange for benefits like safety, order, and justice. This is why we get upset when government officials violate the public trust by mismanaging funds or failing to provide a fair criminal justice system. Participating in society means joining in all sorts of partnerships, whether at our jobs or on our sports teams.

In 1 Corinthians the apostle Paul explains that it's almost impossible to avoid associating with nonbelievers. We would have to leave this world, he says, in order to completely separate ourselves from those who do not claim Christ as Lord (1 Corinthians 5:9-10).

Keep in mind that partnering with nonbelievers does not necessarily mean affirming their beliefs. Esther and Mordecai had to partner with the King of Persia to stop Haman's plan to exterminate the Jewish people (Esther 4–9). Like us, Esther and Mordecai were far from perfect, but God used them to protect his people by engaging the Persian political system and associating with nonbelievers. Esther, in particular, used her influence as queen to nullify the decree that ordered the extermination—at great risk to her own safety (Esther 5:1-7). She put her personal interests aside to follow God's will, courageously saying, "And if I perish, I perish" (Esther 4:16).

Cobelligerents

Partnering with nonbelievers can never mean agreeing with them on all matters. Francis Schaeffer asserted that Christians can't be allied with nonbelievers. He believed an ally must be "a born-again Christian with whom I can go a long way down the road."[4] In other words, we can only fully align with those whose faith we share. However, Schaeffer went on to say that we can work with someone as a cobelligerent, defined as "a person who may not have any sufficient basis for taking the right position, but takes the right position on a single issue. And I can join with him without danger as long as I realize that he's not my ally and all we're talking about is a single issue."[5] It's fair to disagree with Schaeffer's definition of *ally*, but the point remains: we can only share an ultimate objective and alliance with other believers.

Nonbelievers can be wrong about matters of faith and right about a particular issue because of common grace. Nonbelievers may not have the saving grace that comes through faith in Jesus Christ, but everyone is a recipient of God's common grace, which is God's gift to all humankind. The gospel reveals that God "causes his sun to rise on the evil and the good, and sends rain on the righteous and the unrighteous" (Matthew 5:45). "The LORD is good to all; he has compassion on all he has made" (Psalm 145:9), therefore nonbelievers can take part in good works and benefit from them. Christians can partner with others to advance God's will in politics—and society can benefit greatly from the fruit of those partnerships.

Fruitful Partnerships

The civil rights movement is a good example of a partnership that involved Christians and others from different faiths or with no faith at all. Specifically, the Congress of Racial Equity, also known as CORE or the Freedom Riders, brought together groups that included blacks, whites, Christians, Jews, and agnostics. CORE was a civil rights organization engaged in civil disobedience to desegregate the South. Many of the Freedom Riders were college students seeking to garner national attention by disrupting Southern norms and forcing the issue of integration.

They conducted sit-ins at segregated restaurants and broke Jim Crow laws by organizing demonstrations where black people used white-only restrooms. They had one of the more dangerous strategies in the civil rights movement, but they believed it was necessary to get America to pay attention to what was going on in the South. In the early 1960s, CORE tried to force the hand of the Kennedy administration's attorney general, Bobby Kennedy, who wanted them to take a slower and less confrontational posture. The injustice and violence that CORE exposed heightened tensions and embarrassed America internationally.[6] It became clear to other countries that although

America preached freedom and justice, it didn't always practice them at home. The world witnessed wicked events that revealed the sad state of American racism.

In Anniston, Alabama, a group set fire to the Freedom Riders' bus while CORE workers were still inside. In Birmingham, Alabama, Governor Bull Connor gave the Ku Klux Klan fifteen minutes to assault the Freedom Riders with impunity as the FBI watched without interrupting the violence.[7] CORE's efforts, along with those of other civil rights groups, eventually forced the Kennedy administration to federalize the Alabama National Guard to protect the Freedom Riders in the state.

Additionally, partnerships between Christians and non-believers helped pass the Civil Rights Act of 1964 and the Voting Rights Act of 1965. The partnerships included President Lyndon Baines Johnson, who had supported segregation in the past. Diverse coalitions offer strength, and God can use all sorts of people to further his will.

Ideological and Partisan Affiliations

One of the most common political partnerships we enter is with a political party. Whether we formally affiliate with a political party or we're nonmembers or Independents who usually vote for a certain party, we're participating in a form of partnership. We give Democrats or Republicans votes and sometimes resources to represent our interests. While more Americans consider themselves Independent than belong to either political party, America's two-party system is hard for politically active people to avoid.[8] Indeed, most Independents end up aligning with and voting for one of the political parties most of the time anyway. This book won't address whether or not third parties are desirable or viable. Nonetheless, understanding the significance of political parties as partnerships is important.

In theory, parties give our political system a level of structure, especially when it comes to elections. Through platforms, caucuses, and primaries, voters are given the opportunity to select from a group of candidates who generally share their interests and values. Parties recruit and vet the candidates, help raise money, and galvanize groups around certain policy initiatives. In reality, the party system isn't so clean or representative, but many still consider parties to be necessary vehicles for political representation.

In addition to political parties, Americans also affiliate with ideological or cultural tribes, which are less formal. According to the Hidden Tribes of America study, these tribes are group identities that represent core beliefs and reflect the "fundamental ways we understand the world and align ourselves."[9] Over the years, social scientists have "recognized that people see their own groups as a strong source of self-esteem and a sense of belonging. Consequently, these tribal identities have significant influence over people's views."[10]

The study breaks Americans into seven tribes: Progressive Activists, Traditional Liberals, Passive Liberals, Politically Disengaged, Moderates, Traditional Conservatives, and Devoted Conservatives.[11] Interestingly, the two smallest and most extreme tribes (Progressive Activists and Devoted Conservatives, 8 percent and 6 percent of Americans respectively) have the loudest voice in American sociopolitical discourse because of their high levels of engagement and large amounts of money. They often frame the issues for the majority of us, who the study calls the "Exhausted Majority" (67 percent).[12] This has resulted in high levels of polarization.

For Christians, there may well be practical reasons to affiliate with a political party or a tribe, but we run into trouble when we allow that entity to have undue influence on our values and opinions. Some Christians are more willing to defend their ideological tribe than the Christian faith. It's imperative that Christians are deliberate about avoiding partisan and ideological indoctrination. We also compromise our faith when we look to political tribes for validation simply because we want to belong. Our partisan and ideological affiliations should never become religious in nature.

Indoctrination and Validation

In 2014, Brendan Eich was forced to leave Mozilla, the company he led as CEO, because he had donated one thousand dollars to the successful Proposition 8 campaign in California to prohibit same-sex marriage in the state.[13] The previous year, gospel singer Donnie McClurkin withdrew from the fiftieth anniversary of the March on Washington Commemorative Event because of his views and personal story regarding sexual orientation.[14] In 2018, Sarah Riggs Amico, a Democrat running for lieutenant governor in Georgia, was facing pressure to prove her progressive bona fides in the midst of a competitive race, so she released a statement distancing herself from the views of her church. It seems as though she was suggesting that her views on LGBTQ issues were morally superior to those of her own church.[15]

It happens from the political right, too, of course. Pastors have faced pressure from both inside and outside of their churches for speaking out against racism, and Republicans have lost primary challenges for even sporadically challenging the reigning party's orthodoxy. We frequently see political parties and interest groups pressure elected officials to change their opinions on issues of values and justice to stay in step with their party's or groups' agenda. Those who comply may receive funding and exposure. Those who refuse are in some cases targeted and ostracized.

When Christian beliefs aren't popular, our political partners sometimes present us with rewards or punishments to persuade us to surrender our convictions. If we're looking to gain favor or avoid social punishment, we'll likely fail to walk away from the partnership or stand up when necessary. When faced with these predicaments, it's important to remember Jesus' words:

> If the world hates you, keep in mind that it hated me first.
> If you belonged to the world, it would love you as its own.
> As it is, you do not belong to the world, but I have chosen you out of the world. That is why the world hates you. . . .
> They will treat you this way because of my name, for they do not know the one who sent me. (John 15:18-19, 21)

Christians must stand firm in the face of this kind of pressure. Serving God and being faithful to his Word must always be more important than the actions and opinions of the world. Under no circumstances should Christians allow themselves to be indoctrinated by our cobelligerents, nor should we ever seek their validation.

The prophet Daniel provides an exemplary model of how to deal with undue pressure from others. After Babylonia besieged Jerusalem and destroyed the temple, King Nebuchadnezzar took some of the brightest young people out of Jerusalem. He changed their names and taught them his people's language and literature (Daniel 1:1-7). The king was trying to indoctrinate these young people to serve his purposes. He had destroyed all they knew and expected to build them back up in his own image.

Daniel (Belteshazzar), Hananiah (Shadrach), Mishael (Meshach), and Azariah (Abednego) were part of this group. The king offered Daniel a portion of his wine and meat, but Daniel refused to partake because he knew such a meal was in conflict with his beliefs. By refusing to defile himself, Daniel demonstrated that he would not be indoctrinated by any of the king's methods. He drew the line because he had faith in God, was confident in his beliefs, and thought critically. Neither reward nor punishment would make him compromise his conviction.

Shadrach, Meshach, and Abednego took a similar stand when asked to bow to the statute the king created (Daniel 3). Faced with death in a fiery furnace, the men said this:

> King Nebuchadnezzar, we do not need to defend ourselves before you in this matter. If we are thrown into the blazing furnace, the God we serve is able to deliver us from it, and he will deliver us from Your Majesty's hand. But even if he does not, we want you to know, Your Majesty, that we will not serve your gods or worship the image of gold you have set up. (Daniel 3:16-18)

Unfortunately, many Christians fail to respond like Daniel and his friends when confronted by those in power or even by our peers. On certain issues it's almost expected that Christian politicians and civic leaders will endorse policies that directly conflict with their Christian principles. It has become the norm. We allow ourselves to be indoctrinated by political, academic, and pop culture leaders and to surrender our convictions to avoid disassociation and criticism. In many cases our perspective has been so thoroughly shaped—or even discipled—by worldly ideologies that we mistake our flawed ideological positions for Christian positions. When we internalize worldly beliefs, they become the standard or lens through which we discern right and wrong instead of the Bible. We then accept their partisan and ideological positions without taking the time to think critically about them or assess them based on a biblical standard.

For instance, the Democratic Party has gone from supporting the idea that abortions should be "safe, legal, and rare" to enacting laws that remove almost all restrictions and celebrate abortion as a social good.[16] Many Christian Democrats have accepted this position without pushback. Similarly, Republicans such as President Ronald Reagan and George W. Bush talked about immigration policy in much more compassionate terms than Republicans do today. Many Christian Republicans changed their tune once immigration hardliners started threatening the reelection prospects of those who took a more sympathetic approach toward undocumented immigrants. It's easy to buy into the idea that ideological progressives are supposed to think a certain way and conservatives another. We let influencers tell us that if we're smart or patriotic then we'll support whatever point of view they're peddling at the time. That is the definition of indoctrination.

Christians need to embrace an alternative approach, prescribed by the apostle Paul when he instructed followers of Jesus: "Do not conform to the pattern of this world, but be transformed by the renewing of your mind. Then you will be able to test and approve what God's will is—his good, pleasing and perfect will" (Romans 12:2).

Our ability to remain faithful is directly tied to the places we seek and find validation. Seeking validation from a political party, secular elites, or the entertainment industry will easily convince us to abandon our convictions. If we desire the approval of others, then we've empowered them to create the rules and set the standards. The Bible says that many of the religious leaders in Jesus' day believed in him, "but because of the Pharisees they would not openly acknowledge their faith for fear they would be put out of the synagogue; for they loved human praise more than praise of God" (John 12:42-43). When we deny the love or truth of the gospel in order to please others or gain position and power, we deny God and prove that we are most concerned with the approval of people. We squander our inheritance in Christ for worldly treasure.

Do an inventory of where you stand on issues like immigration, criminal justice, abortion, and sexual ethics, and then be honest about how you came to those conclusions. Did you reach your opinions through the love and truth of the Bible or have you been indoctrinated by a group identity that's outside of Christ? Have you relied on the worst arguments and behavior of those you disagree with to avoid considering whether they might have a point? Try to pick at least one issue where you know many Christians disagree with you and commit to earnestly learning why they believe what they believe and consider it. The worst that can happen is that you will better understand your brothers and sisters who disagree with you. And maybe you'll learn something that will sharpen or even change your opinion.

An exercise like this can be very difficult to do on your own, so pray for humility and clarity. You'll likely find that some of your positions shifted when your party or ideological tribe shifted on the issue. Remember, your validation comes from Christ, from whom you've received the ultimate gift: salvation.

Critical Thinking and Questioning Partners

We've all seen someone get called out and chastised by their sociopolitical partners for publicly questioning certain decisions. For example, Republicans get called RINOs (Republican in Name Only) by other Republicans for questioning President Trump's demeaning language and bad behavior. Our partners often try to convince us that our opponents are so evil—and the moment is so urgent—that to question the group's tactics or refuse to endorse its strategies is to do a great disservice to the cause. This is "ends justify the means" thinking that we as Christians cannot accept. Under no circumstances should Christians blindly follow our partners or overlook immorality and bad tactics or strategies for the sake of the movement. We must never surrender our values or forgo critical thinking in our partnerships.

Frederick Douglass, the Christian abolitionist, orator, and writer, understood this quite well. In a lecture in Rochester, New York, he said, "I would unite with anybody to do right and with nobody to do wrong."[17] That quote may seem trite until you understand the context in which Douglass said it. He was explaining that he would partner with the American Anti-Slavery Society to abolish slavery, but he would not partner in their effort to abolish the American government as a whole. They believed the US Constitution was a slaveholding document and that they needed to abolish the Union itself for the sake of emancipation. Douglass disagreed. He understood the flaws in the US Constitution and the blind spots of the founders, but he believed the Constitution opened the door and provided the apparatus to abolish slavery. He said, "To dissolve the Union, as a means to abolish slavery, is about as wise as it would be to burn up this city in order to get the thieves out of it."[18]

No one could credibly claim that Douglass didn't understand the issue or wasn't taking it seriously enough. He had himself been a slave, was separated from his family, and was physically beaten in this demonic institution of slavery, yet Douglass refused to surrender his critical thinking just to appease his partners. This took an incredible amount of fortitude and vision. Remember Douglass the next time your political partners demand that you go along to get along. This man of faith understood that the means of achieving emancipation were not to be overlooked—and history proved him right. Efforts go wrong when people who know better become yes men or women. We hurt the cause most when we fail to be its moral anchor and moral compass.

Cultivating Healthy Partnerships: Practical Steps

Vetting and examining partnerships is imperative when participating in the political arena. Here are some steps to follow when considering or evaluating a cultural or political partnership:

1. Be confident in your identity in Christ. If you're unsure about what you believe or are weak in your convictions, it's important to be honest about that. As Christians mature, we grow stronger in our convictions (Ephesians 4:14-15). Before we step into the public square and partner with others, we must know where we stand on moral issues and be confident enough to defend those stances even if everyone else around us disagrees. If we're not there yet, it doesn't necessarily mean we can't participate in the political process, but we might refrain from joining nonbelievers without guidance from a more mature believer. An impressionable or malleable Christian will more easily take on the positions and posture of their partner. Political ideologies seek converts, and we must be equipped to contend for the faith and avoid conversion to unbiblical value systems.

2. Get to know your partners and understand their endgame. Do your research to understand your partners' ideology and their motivations. Ask them what thinkers they follow and who they model themselves after. If you're teaming up with disciples of William F. Buckley, you should read *God and Man at Yale.* If you're teaming up with Saul Alinsky followers, you should read *Rules for Radicals.* It's also important that you understand your partners' endgame and not just what they are trying to accomplish at the moment. Ask yourself, *What are my partners' ultimate goals in society?* Some Christians attach themselves to efforts that speak of equality and justice, not knowing that the group they've affiliated with believes Christianity is ultimately an obstacle to their ideal society. Don't be blind to your partners' faults and bad traits. You're not going into partnerships to romanticize the relationship; you're going into them to reach a common goal.

3. Identify the objective and shared values. Why are you partnering? What exactly are you trying to achieve? What values do you share? Clearly define the objective and what success looks like. Identify what values you share with your partners. If you want to abolish the cash bail system because you agree that money shouldn't play a role in how long someone is in jail, make sure that's clear to both sides. Don't let that objective and those values drift into other arenas that aren't consistent with Scripture and your convictions. A movement that is initially about social justice can later turn into an effort to remove godly norms and institutions.

4. Identify differences and conflicting views. Make sure you understand what issues you differ on with your partners. You must take account of your differences lest you lose sight of where you stand. Partnering with another group or person should never be seen as an endorsement of their entire agenda. Be clear about what you agree on while emphasizing that you can overcome your differences for the common good. This should be a detailed assessment. For instance, you might both say you support religious freedom, but your partner only supports religious freedom for Christians and not others. You should identify those differences of opinion early in the partnership.

5. Don't isolate the issue. No issue is an island. Every issue affects others, and there can be unintended consequences. You might be called to focus on one issue, while someone else is called to focus on another. Instead of seeing other issues as competition, recognize that there is much work to be done and support the labor of others when you can. Injustices are connected to other injustices anyway: education is tied to the criminal justice system, which is tied to poverty, and so on. We can't focus on every issue, but when we isolate an issue and ignore all others, we can lose perspective and end up damaging our Christian witness.

6. Don't take on your partner's identity. You are a Christian first and foremost. It sounds like a no-brainer, but we often get swallowed up by the movements we participate in and the particular causes we support. Your partners don't validate you or control your opinion. Don't allow your partner to dictate who you converse or fellowship with. To gain control, some groups might try to keep you from connecting with other interests or even other believers. Don't allow anyone to limit your reach. Talk to all interested parties, and don't let your partner be the messenger between you and other groups. For example, in order for Christians of color and white Christians to work together in the public square, they'll have to shed their partisan identities and remove the intermediaries standing between their communication.

7. Protect against losing your identity through active critique. Sociopolitical partnerships are not all-or-nothing propositions. You'll disagree with your partner on certain issues—or at least you should if you haven't taken on their identity. It can be easy for important differences to become subsumed by a partnership, especially a close partnership, unless you reaffirm the convictions behind those differences both to yourself and with your partner. Partnership does not require unanimity on every issue. Anytime someone knows you'll agree with everything they say, they'll very quickly lose respect for you. This is certainly relevant to the situation of Christians in both political parties. To maintain a healthy partnership, Christians must be willing to check their partners and question their tactics and strategies.

Conclusion

Too often Christians have allowed political and partisan associations to compromise biblical convictions. We've allowed our political affiliations to become religious in nature and have followed others into frameworks and actions that run counter to biblical teachings. Christians must be careful about how we engage partners and political parties. If we enter these relationships naively or in need of validation from non-Christians, we can easily lose our Christian identity and end up doing more harm than good.

We must have a strong sense of who we are, what we believe, and what our objectives are before we join hands with nonbelievers in political or social causes. Christians cannot accept the philosophies or tactics of any group uncritically or completely. We must enter politics with a healthy skepticism—always questioning assumptions and evaluating the methods and outcomes of those around us. The civic space is full of hidden agendas and corrupt activity; it's no place to timidly accept the assertions of others. It's intellectually lazy to agree with the same political party on every single issue. That's a clear indication that we've been indoctrinated, which should never be an option for Christians.

CHAPTER FIVE

MESSAGING

RHETORIC

WHAT ARE THEY REALLY SAYING?

The tongue has the power of life and death,
and those who love it will eat its fruit.

PROVERBS 18:21

Christians are called to spread the gospel of Jesus Christ throughout the world by professing the good news of salvation and life in the kingdom of God (Matthew 28:16-20). Accordingly, messaging is a major part of the Christian's mission and daily life. The Bible says, "The soothing tongue is a tree of life, but a perverse tongue crushes the spirit" (Proverbs 15:4). The content of words matters, as does the tone in which Christians address others. Words can lift our spirits, galvanize people for good, or tear down hopes and empires.

Messaging has always been one of Satan's primary weapons as well. In fact, deceitful messaging is partially responsible for the fall of humankind. The enemy deceived Adam and Eve by playing on words and convincing Eve that she would "not certainly die" if she ate the forbidden fruit (Genesis 3:4). In the wilderness, Satan also tried to get Jesus off his mission by using a message that appealed to his flesh (Matthew 4:1-11).

Many of the same tactics are still being used today. Christians are continually urged to disregard the plain directives in the Bible and asked whether the Bible really says that certain things are actually sinful. Christians are tempted to embrace points of view that tickle their ears, justify sins, dehumanize neighbors, and relieve the tension between God's Word and their desires. In politics, groups sometimes reduce complicated matters to simplistic buzzwords to fit their narrative or complicate more straightforward matters to obscure the truth.

The world is constantly bombarding us with well-researched, targeted messaging aimed at persuading, distracting, or enraging us in regard to cultural and political matters. Without a trained eye, it's hard to discern what motives and hidden agendas lie beneath the surface. Christians who fail to dig deeper than the superficial appeal of a message are bound to fall for misdirection and misrepresentations that separate them from God's intentions.

Christians must be wise as snakes and innocent as doves when it comes to cultural and political messaging (Matthew 10:16). Fortunately, the Bible provides examples of how to address others faithfully in the public square. This chapter explores the importance of words and rhetoric in the US political system as well as how to "speak the truth in love" in a culture of deception and rage.

Politics as Rhetoric

In 1933 America was struggling through one of the lowest points of the Great Depression. The stock market had crashed a few years earlier and people all over the nation were out of work, standing in line at soup kitchens, and uncertain about what the future held. Franklin D. Roosevelt, a Harvard-educated man from a wealthy family, had won the 1932 presidential election and was scheduled to give his inaugural address on March 4, 1933. Roosevelt was known for his charisma and sense of humor, but he wasn't known as an orator or policymaker of any great depth. However, at a time when Americans needed inspiration, leadership, and a path forward, Roosevelt gave what is considered one of the greatest speeches of the twentieth century. He famously told the country:

> This great Nation will endure as it has endured, will revive and prosper. So, first of all, let me assert my firm belief that the only thing to fear is fear itself—nameless, unreasoning, unjustified terror which paralyzes needed efforts to convert retreat into advance. In every dark hour of national life a leadership of frankness and vigor has met with the understanding and support of the people themselves which is essential to victory. I am convinced that you will again give that support to leadership in these critical days.[1]

With his words, Roosevelt aroused a spirit of hope and endurance in the American people as well as trust in a presidency that was just starting. While some people may disagree with the policies he pursued to get the country out of the Great Depression, his ability to lift the spirits of the American people with speeches and his fireside chats was unquestionable. Roosevelt's contemporaries, Adolf Hitler in Germany and Joseph Stalin in the Soviet Union, took the opposite approach. They decided to galvanize their people through hatred, scapegoating, and unspeakable cruelty. Leaders throughout history have used their bully pulpits to rouse the best and the worst in people.

Communication is a major factor in our political system. As the Roosevelt example demonstrates, a strong communicator whose finger is on the pulse of society can stir people's passions and garner great influence. Finely tuned rhetoric is an invaluable form of political capital needed to push ideas and policy forward.

American philosopher Richard J. Burke believed American politics is best understood as rhetoric. Burke argued that in the political arena, we gain influence through symbols and communication that are "conscious attempts . . . to persuade other people (audience) to adopt particular attitudes." He emphasized the attempt to persuade, which is different from compelling others to adopt certain positions and attitudes. Burke says that an attempt to persuade "risks failure to persuade and thus recognizes his freedom as a human being to make up his own mind."[2] In general, our influence depends on our ability to persuade others. Political elections are full of attempts to gain support through the art of speaking and writing.

Debates are an opportunity to hear candidates address one another's ideas, qualifications, and past actions. This is a much better option than determining our leaders through duels or bloodlines. In authoritarian countries such as North Korea and Russia, a political leader's ability to persuade is virtually inconsequential because free speech is censored.

The Bible affirms the value of persuasion. In Acts 17, the apostle Paul went to the agora in Athens, where the best philosophers and debaters came to match wits and exchange ideas.[3] Socrates and Plato spoke at agoras during their lifetimes.[4] The apostle Paul saw the value in bringing the gospel to a place where ideas flourished. Tim Keller explains that Paul "believed that the gospel had what it took to engage the thinking public, the cultural elites, and to challenge the cultural ideas of the days."[5] It's clear that Paul came into that environment prepared. The Bible says he reasoned in the marketplace as he engaged in dialogue.[6] He understood the spirit of the day and even used Athenian rhetorical devices to get his point across.[7] Keller further explains that what Paul says is "deeply biblical, but he never quotes the Bible, instead he shows them the weakness and inadequacies of their own view."[8]

Paul's words and posture in the agora are instructive for believers to engage the sociopolitical arena. Paul shows that effectively engaging nonbelievers takes more than quoting Scripture to people who don't believe in its authority. Christians should understand the subject matter and articulate biblical principles in terms that resonate with the audience. It's unfortunate when believers are passionate about their opinions yet aren't informed or able to clearly articulate their point of view. This is not how Christians should conduct themselves when they go about the Father's business in the public square. Well-prepared believers can do great work for Christ with words.

In the early stages of creating what would become the AND Campaign, we sought opportunities to engage the political arena in clever ways. In June of 2014, the US Supreme Court ruled on the *Burwell v. Hobby Lobby* case, which focused on whether or not closely held corporations could be forced to pay for certain types of contraception that some consider to be the equivalent of abortion.[9] Based on the Religious Freedom Restoration Act the court ruled that Hobby Lobby and similar corporations could not be forced to do so. Many progressives argued that women's health had been disregarded and that as a result of this decision women all over the country would be left without contraception.

A few days later the Young Democrats of Atlanta hosted a forum to discuss the subject. We saw this as the perfect opportunity to speak into the public square with love and truth. Justin Giboney and a few other attorneys reviewed the decision and legal expert commentaries and created a summary in layman's terms for the rest of the AND Campaign team. The team studied the summary and went to the forum prepared for the discussion. The panel included people from Planned Parenthood and other far-left groups, and as we suspected, there was a lot of emotion and conjecture, though no one on the panel seemed to have read the actual legal opinion. After allowing the panelists to have their say, our team began to ask questions and break down the true implications of the ruling for the audience. We even quoted some progressive legal scholars who predicted that the effect of the ruling wouldn't be as drastic as many of their peers suggested. By the end of the forum more people were directing their questions toward us than the actual panel. A local judge in the audience emailed us the next day, saying that she was impressed by our knowledge of the subject matter and that she had learned more about the case from us. We made a lasting impression on behalf of the body of Christ in what could have been a hostile environment.

You can serve your community in this way too. Here are some guidelines for faithful and effective communication in the public square:

1. *Study and be confident.* To persuade others in the public square, as Christians we first have to be confident in our convictions, and confidence comes from knowing what we believe and why we believe it. Study Scripture and read the thoughts of orthodox writers on pressing topics in society.

2. *Show love and concern.* We as Christians must genuinely love the people we're addressing. We have wasted a lot of time trying to correct those to whom we haven't shown true concern. Why should others listen to us if we're talking down to them or failing to show them compassion? If we're not demonstrating humility and sincere social concern, our words will fall flat.

3. *Be informed.* Do research. To be effective we must understand the subject matter and understand the mood of our audience. We must thoroughly understand our own point of view and our interlocutor's.

4. *Have a plan.* We should anticipate how those receiving our message will engage and the questions they'll have. It's helpful to plot our points of interaction and our responses ahead of time.

5. *Maintain a hopeful, positive tone.* We shouldn't walk into a conversation with people with different beliefs and assume they'll automatically agree with us. Instead, Christians should anticipate their disagreements and keep our composure as we speak in a way that glorifies God.

6. *Relate to the audience.* We should speak in terms our audience understands and use sources they respect whenever possible. It's possible to communicate biblical principles without actually quoting the Bible.

7. *Be persuasive.* It's important to take the time to think through the logic of our argument—its premises and conclusions. We

should be prepared to walk our audience toward our conclusion without assuming too much and without insulting their intelligence, using illustrations and symbols they can relate to.

8. ***Don't hide your convictions.*** Sometimes we're so self-conscious about not sounding harsh or judgmental that no one knows what we actually believe. That's ineffective and often demonstrates a lack of courage. It's possible to "speak the truth in love" and to be winsome without hiding Christian convictions. Remember, the Holy Spirit ultimately brings people to Christ, not our charm or persuasive arguments.

Language and Politics

The Ephesians 4:14 reference to "the cunning and craftiness of people in their deceitful scheming" sounds like a perfect description of the tactics used in political discourse today. Political parties and interest groups spend millions of dollars on research and messaging to influence opinions and to cause certain reactions. Disinformation campaigns and propaganda are nothing new. Since the beginning of time, messaging has been used to manipulate as those with hidden agendas stretch the truth and mislead people for their own purposes.

In 1946, the English writer George Orwell wrote a famous essay titled "Politics and the English Language." The essay describes how words are used and abused in politics and beyond. Orwell believed the English language was in decline, partially because of "political causes." In his estimation language was suffering because "political speech and writing are largely a defence of the indefensible. . . . Politics itself is a mass of lies, evasion, folly [and] hatred."[10]

Not all politicians are dishonest, but too often they play on words or use misdirection instead of telling the truth, the whole truth, and nothing but the truth. It's happened in presidential administrations that each party holds in high esteem. During the Iran-Contra scandal, President Ronald Reagan's administration was caught lying about the US government selling weapons to Iran in violation of an embargo. And many still remember President Bill Clinton's infamous words during the Monica Lewinsky trial: "I did not have sexual relations with that woman." Both parties also frequently have moments when they have compromised the truth to accomplish political ends or simply to avoid legal or electoral consequences.

The most effective political slogans are short (they can fit on a bumper sticker) and play on words and symbols that are meaningful to the audience. A strong political message resonates with its listeners and makes well-defined images pop up in their heads. Slogans such as "It's Morning Again in America," "It's the Economy, Stupid," "Change We Can Believe In," and "Make America Great Again" each connected with key demographics and led to political victories. As Shakespeare wrote in *Hamlet*, "brevity is the soul of wit"—but it's not always the keeper of substance or intellectual honesty.

In a section of Orwell's essay labeled "Meaningless Words," he explains how in politics words "are often used in a consciously dishonest way. That is, the person who uses them has his own private definition, but allows the hearer to think he means something quite different."[11] Orwell lists words such as *patriotic, freedom, equality*, and *progressive* as being particularly prone to deceptive use. People generally attach a positive value to those words, but they're actually quite vague and often purposely used in absence of a clear and detailed explanation. A speaker talking about *freedom* might really be proposing the removal of needed regulations or decreasing corporate accountability. A speaker using the word *equality* might actually be advocating for the rejection of biological differences between men and women rather than equitable treatment. And what does it mean when a candidate says their policy is the most *progressive* or *conservative*? Statements like these are often applauded, but they can be completely meaningless in regard to gauging the quality of the proposed solution.

When we hear a catchy phrase with such words in it, how should we react? We shouldn't react at all until we understand the context and how the word is being applied to the topic of discussion. We shouldn't let speakers get a reaction out of us by simply using cheap buzzwords that mean virtually nothing. Speakers insult our intelligence when they use vague terms and expect us to be easily pleased or enraged. Neither our approval nor our indignation should be so easily accessible. We should have a healthy skepticism and ask for an explanation. We will likely be surprised how often we will find empty words hidden behind smoke and mirrors. It's better to completely ignore these slogans than to base our political decisions on skillfully phrased hot air.

A name doesn't always accurately describe something's essence or intentions. As millennials well know, Sallie Mae sounds like a sweet and benevolent grandmother until the student loan bank garnishes your wages. Christians should be careful not to judge an organization or legislation by its name. Many of the groups and policies we regularly encounter have names that arouse a certain emotion or impression in us but don't accurately represent them in substance. This is akin to false advertising, which can be so untruthful that Congress passed the Wheeler-Lea Act in 1938 and established the National Advertising Review Board in 1971 to protect consumers from deception.[12] Unfortunately, much less is done to protect citizens in the political arena and the marketplace of ideas from misleading branding.

Who wouldn't support the Patriot Act or the Equality Act? Those names sound so pure and honorable. However, critics would say the Patriot Act invades the privacy of Americans by allowing the government to have access to our information and activities in unconstitutional ways. Highly regarded legal scholars believe the Equality Act would dismantle important aspects of religious liberty, leaving churches and faith-based hospitals and colleges exposed to litigation they don't have the resources to fight. Whether we support those policies or not, we must admit that the names don't describe the complex and far-reaching effects of the actual legislation. A lot of people who have publicly supported those policies probably haven't even heard the criticisms. They're simply focused on the words and the groups that support the policies.

Imagine being in the middle of a campaign and hearing your political opposition say, "She didn't support the Equality Act!" You'd likely lose the crowd immediately, with no time to explain the true impact of the legislation. Interest groups know that's an elected official's worst nightmare, which incentivizes office-holders to take the easy path and support the legislation. But this gimmick only works on uninformed voters who rely on vague words and phrases. Don't be that voter.

In political advocacy, a shortcut to building a longstanding brand that people trust and appreciate is to attach your effort to a movement that already has high standing. This explains why many modern secular movements co-opt the language of the civil rights movement while discarding the faith that led and fueled the activists in that effort. Liberals and conservatives use the words of Martin Luther King Jr. and Fannie Lou Hamer with hopes of improving their own reputations without really embodying the true spirit of the civil rights movement. Don't fall for it. Every campaign and movement must be appraised based on its own works and the merit of its agenda.

Oversimplifying Issues

Political messaging often aims to obscure more complex realities. A brilliant but dishonest slogan can reduce a difficult matter into a black or white moral question.

In the 1980s, America was dealing with the crack epidemic and the wave of violence that came along with it. The far-reaching impacts of crack were ravaging communities all over America, eventually forcing the federal government to take action. The response was to resume what President Nixon had coined the "War on Drugs." The enactment of mandatory minimum prison sentences and other harsh criminal justice measures sent record numbers of African American and Hispanic men to prison for extended periods. The initiative devastated already suffering communities by greatly increasing the prison population and leaving more innocent children fatherless. Framing the epidemic in terms of war contributed to a posture that became an attack on families and communities of color rather than just a fight against illegal substances.

The "War on Drugs" was coupled with programs like the "Just Say No" antidrug campaign aimed at discouraging children from illegal drug use. The program was well-meaning, but the slogan reflected and perpetuated an attitude that reduced the crack epidemic to a simple yes or no choice. It overlooked factors such as poverty, inequality, and racism that drove depressed and discouraged people to drug use. Drug users could simply be seen as morally bankrupt losers. In many instances this led to a lack of compassion for poor communities and a harsher criminal justice system, which we're still trying to fix decades later. While we should be careful not to completely relieve individuals of personal responsibility, reducing drug addiction to a casual choice was certainly not an accurate depiction of the crack epidemic any more than it is of today's heroin epidemic.

Perhaps no issue is filled with more misleading taglines and false narratives than the abortion debate. For decades both sides have tested out messaging to sway public opinion in their direction. One side often neglects the tough situations women face, while the other elevates personal choice over human dignity. In particular, sayings such as "My Body, My Choice" and framing abortion as a "women's health" issue have stripped the conversation of essential considerations, completely removing the child's life from the equation. Those who support more restrictive abortion laws than what we currently have (a category that includes a diverse group of women) are characterized as "anti-women" and accused of being motivated by a desire to control women with no regard for their health or well-being. That narrative creates the perfect heartless villain—but it just isn't truthful.

Without a doubt, the United States should do more to address the issues that drive many women to have an abortion, including poverty, abuse, and health care disparities. There should also be a robust effort to reduce maternal mortality rates generally, and among black women especially. That said, to pretend that this matter doesn't also involve the body and life of a human baby is intellectually dishonest. Many pro-choice advocates completely disregard the life of the baby and their slogans help people avoid wrestling with that reality. Even if the heart is beating and the baby is kicking and viable, their narrative can't allow the baby to be considered at all. Acknowledging another living person in their story line would complicate what they've tried to make a straightforward women's health versus women haters scenario.

Clever messaging should not prompt Christians to ignore a human life made in the image of God. Both the health and body of women and the health and body of the child should be considered. Anything less is untruthful.

The more important the issue, the less Christians should rely on talking points and taglines. If our assessment is limited to the resonance of a phrase, then we've outsourced our thought process to well-paid wordsmiths. Regurgitating buzzwords is easy and careless. Next time you discuss hot-button issues such as poverty or abortion, ask all parties involved to avoid slogans and to explain their point of view without using jargon. That'll test whether everyone really knows why they believe what they preach.

What to Do with Religious Rhetoric

In American politics religious rhetoric has been used for many purposes such as aligning one's policies with moral authority and winning the support of religious people. The reasons range from the nefarious to the earnest. Religious rhetoric has sometimes been a part of the very best of political expression, such as in Abraham Lincoln's second inaugural address, when he charged,

> With malice toward none, with charity for all, with firmness in the right as God gives us to see the right, let

us strive on to finish the work we are in, to bind up the nation's wounds, to care for him who shall have borne the battle and for his widow and his orphan, to do all which may achieve and cherish a just and lasting peace among ourselves and with all nations.[13]

Religious rhetoric can be used to mislead and cover up evil. This is why it is particularly important that believers are not easily tickled by empty religious slogans or appeals. Christians do not listen to politicians in order to be affirmed or even to hear politicians express beliefs they share. Instead, we listen to politicians because their words provide us with leverage to hold them accountable. If a political leader talks about how important Christianity is in this country, we should not reward the politician because they have flattered us. At best, politicians' words might be meaningful to the extent they view a positive role for faith in public life for the good of all people.

In 1999, in the run-up to the his election victory in 2000, George W. Bush told a gathering of Southern Baptists, "I've heard the call. I believe God wants me to be president."[14] During her 2016 presidential campaign, Hillary Clinton spoke at the National Baptist Convention USA's 136th General Conference and, citing Micah 6:8, told Christians there that "we need a president who will do justice, love kindness and walk humbly with our God."[15] This kind of rhetoric can be important and meaningful if it is used to hold an elected leader accountable. However, if we as Christians are listening to politicians in order to be flattered or to personally identify with a politician, then we will be easily manipulated. A politician's job is not to listen to the same music we do or use the same kind of language we

do. And if a modern campaign is sharing that kind of information, it is often attempting to get credit for something un-
related to the actual job the candidate seeks.

Christians shouldn't chase after the plaudits of politicians; we
receive our reward in Christ. We're interested in politics for the
same reason our elected officials should be: to serve the public.

Dehumanizing Opponents

In 1974, George Bliss of the *Chicago Tribune* coined the term
welfare queen to describe a woman who took advantage of government assistance.[16] While there are always people who use
any system dishonestly, this term became a widespread cari-
cature that stigmatized all women who used food stamps and
other government programs. Women who were just trying to
keep their children from starving were viewed with suspicion
and disdain. And the term had a practical impact on American
policy as well. Conservative politicians used the label to criticize
social programs in general. The suggestion was that supporting
welfare was to enable welfare queens. Sadly, this narrative de-
humanized an entire demographic of people who were worthy
of compassion and respect.

As Christians, we have to be careful about how we label
people. When we portray others in a demeaning light, we sin
against them and reveal our own lack of wisdom (Proverbs
11:12). Discrediting a group might help us win an argument, but
if it belittles our neighbor, it's wrong. Moreover, we should directly
and vocally reject descriptors that disparage others, including
our political opponents. Today, humiliating our opposition and
depicting them as spawns of pure evil is an accepted—and
successful—political tactic.

Political leaders often talk as if their side is for all that is good and true, and the other side is for death and destruction. But civic decisions become too easy when we as Christians pretend politics is simply a battle between angels and demons. The implication is that we don't have to parse the details of their proposals or weigh the alternatives, we just need to know what position the "right side" is taking. This makes for a simple and powerful narrative, but in a broken world, neither side is completely good.

There weren't any perfect groups of people in the Bible (Romans 3:23), and there is only one perfect human, Jesus Christ (Isaiah 53:9). That fact still stands today. That isn't to say that both sides of any given issue are equal or that one side can't be clearly wrong, but a quick look at the record of any party or tribe will dispel all misconceptions about their infallibility. Indeed, sometimes political opponents are plainly misguided or even ill intended, and we as Christians would be remiss not to correct them. However, we must be able to disagree and work against those with opposing beliefs without dehumanizing them. When we label other groups evil, stupid, or irredeemable—or deny their pain—we strip them of their human dignity and make ourselves and others less likely to show them concern and compassion.

The command to love your enemies (Matthew 5:44) must apply to the way we as Christians characterize people or groups who do terrible things. Otherwise, we're susceptible to become just like the people who hurt us. The Bible says, "If you love those who love you, what credit is that to you? Even sinners love those who love them. And if you do good to those who are good to you, what credit is that to you? Even sinners do that" (Luke 6:32-33). Even groups who perpetuate injustice deserve to be treated humanely. Failing to recognize this can result in an even greater evil.

For example, there's no question that in the nineteenth century, the Russian authorities who controlled what's now the country of Georgia often treated the peasant class unfairly and harshly.[17] Joseph Stalin, who grew up as one of those peasants, opposed them. His community had suffered under their rule for too long. However, that doesn't mean Stalin was justified or had a valid reason to demonize the Russians, leading to the murder of tens of millions of people, including women and children. Once he characterized the Russians as less than human because of their past actions, he opened the door to denying their worth entirely. Hatred can make genocide seem like a good deed. Some believe that victims are always justified in how they punish the victimizer, but that's not biblical. Many of the world's biggest monsters started off as victims but did even greater injustices themselves when the power was in their hands.

Conversely, Harriet Tubman and Frederick Douglass experienced the evils of slavery firsthand and worked toward abolition without dehumanizing or calling for reciprocal treatment of white society. Fannie Lou Hamer lived through the oppression of the Jim Crow South and was beaten at the request of Mississippi authorities for no good reason. But when asked how she felt about the perpetrator, she showed him compassion instead of dehumanizing his entire tribe.[18]

Conclusion

Jesus listened to the weak and marginalized (John 4:1-42). Accordingly, Christian political engagement shouldn't be all about what Christians have to say. We should go out of our way to make sure the voiceless are heard and respected. Too often those without money or organized numbers are ignored and underrepresented. If one of our primary objectives in politics is to protect others, then we have to hear their perspectives and concerns without assuming we already know what's best for them.

Similarly, we don't need to eliminate opposing views. The religious leaders in Jerusalem tried to silence the apostles and misrepresent their words because they feared the truth (Acts 4:1-22). Oppressive regimes do the same thing to maintain their false narratives and avoid being exposed. We don't want to be guilty of extinguishing credible counterpoints because they challenge us. Sadly, instead of developing better arguments, some elements of American society are trying to prevent their opponents from speaking. By canceling and deplatforming dissenting voices, they claim to be keeping people safe, but they're really just keeping their ideas from being examined publicly. Christians should want others to examine our testimony. We don't need to avoid debate. We need to study, listen to others, and sharpen our message. Race, sex, socioeconomic status, or political party doesn't disqualify anyone from entering a discussion; the substance of a person's argument is what's important.

Choose your words wisely and remember that when you speak in the public square, you're going about your Father's business. Christian messaging should always be rooted in the gospel.

CHAPTER SIX

POLITICS

RACE

Regardless of race, Christians all serve the same God and have the same Great Commission, the same Great Requirement, and the same commitment to love and truth. Yet somehow we as Christians struggle to find common ground. The church is made of many parts but one body, meaning we are meant to work, worship, and fellowship together regardless of race, culture, or class (Romans 12:4-5; 1 Corinthians 12:12-27; Galatians 3:28).

Unfortunately, the American church has always been divided along racial lines. There are exceptions, but generally we struggle to see past racial and cultural differences and treat each other like brothers and sisters in Christ. This continues to severely damage the church's credibility. How can we speak healing into a broken world when we are reflecting the world's divides?

In actual fact the deep racial divides in our nation present one of the greatest opportunities for the American church. Racism is in the church, but it is not unique to the church. It's the gospel that is unique to the church—the truth that the divine power of Almighty God reaches even across the deepest of cultural divides (Romans 1:16). While other systems and institutions struggle to face this greatest of American challenges, the church should be leading the way. Our capacity to move beyond racism to true unity should be one of the greatest testaments to the reality that God is at work among us (John 13:35).

A lack of knowledge about American history, racism embedded in ideological perspectives, and the continued effects of racism and racist policies prevents us from pursuing true racial reconciliation. Racial reconciliation is a process that starts with the gospel and ends with the gospel. If we are unwilling to become informed and push back against our tribes when they are racially insensitive or manipulative, we will continue to fall well short of God's intention for us.

History of Racism and the American Church

God has presented an ethnically diverse vision of the church from the very first day of its existence. (No fewer than fifteen different ethnic groups are identified hearing the gospel proclaimed in their own tongue on the day of Pentecost in Acts 2.) But even in the early church racial injustice threatened the harmony of the body of Christ. Race-based discrimination in the service of early Christian widows gave rise to the service of deacons in the church in Acts 6. Simply put, the American church was not the first group of Christians to struggle with issues of race.

The American church does, however, have a long and unique story of struggle with racism. That story begins with the nation's original sin of slavery. As the system of owning human beings as chattel property grew in America, so too did the need to deal with some of the troubling contradictions slavery presented for a community (and eventually a nation) largely rooted in Christian principles and oriented around the idea of liberty. As is well stated by historian Paul Harvey, "Once slavery took root in the Americas, it was inevitable that religious authorities would decree that, if slavery existed, God must have a reason for it—and that reason must be in the Bible."[1] Many of America's founding fathers were themselves both devout Christians and slaveholders. Most did not make any public, biblical defense of the institution. This might have had less to do with any wholesale opposition to the institution of slavery and more to do with the assumption of its acceptability. Writ large, the early American church silently condoned the demonic institution of slavery. And some, such as Baptist theologian Richard Fuller, actively defended and perpetuated it.[2] This silence continued on the part of much of the church beyond American slavery and through the Jim Crow era. Martin Luther King Jr. was still combating tacit acceptance of racial injustice in his "Letter from a Birmingham Jail" in 1963.

This history is important to bear in mind as Christians consider how the church can move forward on a road to racial reconciliation, including and especially as it relates to civic and political issues. Religious liberty is one of the key principles that precipitated the establishment of the American colonies and eventually the United States. And yet the American church has historically forced black people to worship separately and sometimes in secret.

In his book *Slave Religion*, Albert Raboteau explains that many slaves were forbidden to attend church or even pray. For a black slave to pursue meaningful religious experience was to risk flogging. As a consequence, slaves would have clandestine worship meetings in hidden locations at opportune times, unbeknownst to slaveholders. This would become known as the "Invisible Institution."[3]

Racism was pervasive even among Christians who did not own slaves or advocate for slavery. White evangelicals such as Henry Ward Beecher played a significant role in the American abolitionist movement. But Beecher and others did not advocate the full inclusion and equality of African Americans in society or in the church.[4] When Christian denominations split over the issue of slavery, the antislavery denominations of the north did not welcome black people as equal participants in fellowship.[5]

E. Franklin Frazier relates an account from 1787 that involved one such northern church:

> When the number of Negroes attending St. George Methodist Episcopal Church increased, Negroes were removed from the seats around the wall and ordered to sit in the gallery. Mistaking the section of the gallery which they were to occupy, Richard Allen, Absalom Jones, and another member were almost dragged from their knees as they prayed. They left the church and together with other Negro members founded the Free African Society. . . . The movement begun by Allen under the name of African societies spread to other cities where so-called African Methodist Episcopal Churches were set up.[6]

Racism has affected American society, and it has deeply affected the American church. As Christians pursue reconciliation, we must be willing to confront the racist history not only of the nation but also of the church itself. The gospel provides grace for this. And the Scriptures provide profound guidance.

Confronting Racism

> Now when Peter had come to Antioch, I withstood him to
> his face, because he was to be blamed; for before certain men
> came from James, he would eat with the Gentiles; but when
> they came, he withdrew and separated himself, fearing those
> who were of the circumcision. And the rest of the Jews also
> played the hypocrite with him, so that even Barnabas was
> carried away with their hypocrisy. (Galatians 2:11-13 NKJV)

Race is a part of the history of the United States and a part
of the history of the church. Many of the personal and corporate
experiences of Christians with race have been shameful and
hurtful. Race is not an easy topic to engage, but an unwillingness
to confront the issue of racism is one of the greatest roadblocks
to reconciliation.

In Galatians 2:11-13, Paul confronts his fellow apostle Peter.
Peter received a powerful vision from heaven, which helped him
understand that God had accepted the Gentiles into the fellowship of the Lord Jesus. Peter, having received this revelation,
had begun to eat and build community with the Gentiles.
However, Jewish Christians from Jerusalem had not yet received
the revelation, and they still rejected Gentile believers. When
these Judaizers arrived, Peter hypocritically shunned the Gentiles. His behavior was shameful and, above all, damaging to the
Christian fellowship. And it would have gone unchecked and
uncorrected had Paul not called it out. This principle holds for
our dealings with the difficult issue of racism in America and in
the American church. Christians can't get right, and we can't be
reconciled, unless we call out racism.

We must confront racism with humility and grace, with a
posture of self-examination, not self-defense, remembering that

God demands something of all of us (Exodus 20), even if we've been the victim. As Christians we ought to have a much clearer view of our own depravity and need for mercy. That awareness of sin in our lives and in our own cultures must drive us to a posture of humility, first toward God and then by extension to our fellow humans (Ephesians 5:21). Furthermore, being aware of the profound mercy and forgiveness of God, we should find grace to confront our personal and cultural issues knowing that we serve a God of love who intends to cleanse us from sin rather than to destroy us because of it (1 John 1:9).

The colorblind ideology that says "I don't see race" should not be embraced by Christians. When we choose to look past race, we also choose to avert our eyes from the many ways that even well-meaning people and institutions engage in practices that reproduce and reinforce negative outcomes such as segregation, disadvantages for minorities in the job market, and the portrayal of whiteness as superior in public communications and entertainment. The simple fact is that if we can't see and discuss the issue of race, we cannot solve the problems that racism causes. When we see that black American preschoolers are 3.6 times more likely to be suspended from school than their white counterparts, colorblindness asks us to search for some rational explanation other than racial discrimination.[7] Colorblind ideology can cause a form of denial in which we're unwilling to acknowledge race as the root cause of tough issues because we don't want to admit that we still have work to do. We have to come to terms with America's race issue by honestly examining ourselves and our institutions.

But the greater danger in the colorblind ideology is that it misses the heart of God where race is concerned. Even in John's vision of the redeemed in heaven, he was able to perceive racial and cultural distinctions (Revelation 7:9 10). Race is not just the color of our skin—as 1 John 3:2 says, we do not yet know what we will be—but according to John, whatever we will be, we will still bear these glorious distinctions. Jesus Christ has opened a way for believers to bring all of our brokenness—even our racial brokenness—before the throne of God and there find help (Hebrews 4:16). We must confront racism in a way that keeps racial diversity intact. In Christ, racial diversity can be redeemed.

Identity Politics: Coupling of the Racial and Sociopolitical Divide

Identity politics is a form of political engagement that puts a particular characteristic or sociological affiliation (such as one's race, ethnicity, religion, gender, or sexuality) as a determinative and exclusive indicator of one's political positions. Identity politics assumes that people who share a certain characteristic will have a shared, common interest and a unique, exclusive perspective that should serve as the basis for political involvement. Identity politics is often based on conceptions of group interest rather than universal principle.

An overdependence on identity politics can be unhealthy. It can be a hurdle to thinking about politics in an other-centered way, and when institutionalized it can cloud individual agency or illegitimate leaders can become recognized spokespersons. Identity politics can also flatten the human experience. Clearly, there is not a perfect overlap between identity and politics; people who share an identity disagree about politics all of the time and view their own self-interest differently. Still, the basic conclusion that identity should be a factor when considering what political alliances to form or who to support is not unfounded.

This is particularly true when it comes to race. For hundreds of years race has been used as one of the primary reasons for exclusion in American society. In the formative centuries of American civic life, race prevented certain people from joining the various mainstream institutions that make up civil society and channel political power. Indeed, it is not altogether inaccurate to suggest that the first people and institutions to participate in identity politics were the mainstream institutions and the people who led them. In this environment of exclusion the minority community formed formal institutions such as churches and civic leagues as well the informal civic framework.

Race-based exclusion created identity politics, and the experiences of marginalized groups in America have reinforced it. The basic, primal kinship that one can feel toward other people of the same race plays a part in identity politics: a black man wants to be able to show his son another successful black man as evidence that he can also be great. To conclude that your interests won't be fully represented when no one making the decisions looks like you or shares your experience is a logical deduction with a sound historical basis.

Identity is a powerful force in American society; it galvanizes and drives people in ways that few other issues can. We have to be aware that any time such power is available, political opportunists will come up with ways to manipulate and exploit it. Politics is tricky that way.

But life is more complicated than identity politics often suggests. People's motives or character can't be determined based on their race or gender alone. There are people of good faith and people of bad faith, and qualified and incompetent people in every demographic. And true commitment to our values requires a deeper level of analysis than intersectionality if we hope to see those values advocated by the people we choose to represent us.

And again, the church should be leading the way. We can understand and appreciate identity politics, intersectionality, and critical race theory. But our identity is in Christ, and our political values are deeply rooted in our faith. This should help us avoid identity-based manipulation at the hands of political parties and political leaders.

Tribalism: Beneficiaries of the Divide

In Acts 19, a man named Demetrius stirred up the people of Ephesus into a riot. Paul had been there preaching the gospel, and many had been saved. These converts had abandoned their worship of the goddess Diana. Demetrius, by making exaggerated and unreasonable claims about the livelihood of the businesspeople and cultural respect, stirred the anger of the people until they had turned into a mob. And why did Demetrius do this? He was a silversmith who made personalized statues of the goddess Diana, and the preaching of the gospel was cutting into his profits.

In society there are always people who benefit from confusion and division. Unfortunately, American politics have some interests that benefit from Christianity's racial divide. Like Demetrius in Ephesus, some people are willing to stoke the flames of racial division with baseless and exaggerated claims. The goal of this kind of behavior is to turn a group of people into a mob. A mob can passionately seek an outcome without ever gaining clarity about why it is seeking that outcome in the first place. As we learn with Demetrius's mob in Acts, "Some were shouting one thing, some another. Most of the people did not even know why they were there" (Acts 19:32). There was chaos and confusion, and the only thing that people were sure about and agreed on was that they were angry. Some of the people in Christian tribes want us to be divided and stirred into chaos because it makes it easier for them to control the opinions of large numbers of people.

Christians have to avoid mobs. We must be adept at identifying people who are trying to stir a group of people into one. Before we throw ourselves into a group, we should apply some analysis to discern whether we are joining a passionate, positive coalition or a destructive mob by asking ourselves the following:

1. Am I clear on the objective of this group or leader and why it's important? Are the other people in the group also clear?

2. Is the rhetoric of this group or leader based on exaggerated claims and baseless accusations against others or on a solid, proactive rationale?

3. Am I allowed to ask questions?

4. Is the group acting out of love for our neighbors?

5. Do we listen and respond to people who disagree?

By thinking critically and loving our neighbor, we can avoid the influence of mobs that thrive off of division.

Steps Toward Racial Reconciliation: It's a Process

Reconciliation is the ending of hostility, disunity, and dissociation in favor of peaceful relations. True reconciliation doesn't happen overnight. And it is a process that can't rightly be conceived of until we're fully committed to winning the fight against racism and attending to the many disparities that racism has created. All this makes civic and political engagement a ripe environment for a process of reconciliation to unfold. This space already calls for relationship building. Forming new coalitions is a primary approach to building new power. And when Christians add their unique contributions to this work of intentionality around reconciliation, amazing things can happen.

The miracle of reconciliation can unfold as Christians move through a four-step process, yet this process is relational, not formulaic. It depends much more on the condition of our hearts than fidelity to the rules. It relies on the power of the Holy Spirit to make it work, not our ability to do so.

STEPS TO RACIAL RECONCILIATION

STEP 1: AWARENESS

Description: Christians have to understand the history of race in America. Many of us don't have the entire story, and our understanding of race is built on false narratives.

Practical Action: Your church can host an educational event about race in America. It should be done by a group or speaker who is frank about the damage racism has done but also aspirational.

STEP 2: RELATIONSHIPS

Description: As long as we continue to deal with one another through caricatures and messengers with ulterior motives, we'll struggle to see eye to eye. We must be deliberate about building personal relationships and understanding.

Practical Action: Host a series of conversations (or a fellowship event) with a church whose demographics are substantially different from yours. Share life stories and then begin to discuss race.

STEP 3: ADVOCACY

Description: From criminal justice to religious liberty, there are some issues that all Christians should be fighting for regardless of their partisan affiliation. When we're able to advocate side by side for issues based on Christian principles, we'll begin to see our common ground and common interest.

Practical Action: Connect with a church or churches whose demographics are substantially different from yours. Identify an issue that your partner church is concerned with or has advocated for and you have not, and then do some advocacy actions together on that issue. Next time, ask them to join you in advocating for an issue. (For example, this could be a church that has never advocated for criminal justice reform joining a partner church on that issue.)

STEP 4: ACTIVE RECONCILIATION

Description: Begin to pursue mutual wholeness and flourishing based on a new understanding of mutual submission and shared resources.

Practical Action: Meet together to identify assets and needs on both sides of the relationship. Challenge yourself to both give and receive. Start small and grow from there.

CHAPTER SEVEN

ADVOCACY

PROTEST

Our Lord describes his disciples in the Sermon on the Mount as salt and light in a dark and dying world (Matthew 5:13). We are called to be a preserving element in society. Salt cannot prevent rottenness, but it does serve to slow the process of going bad. As light, we are expected to be a source of moral clarity and biblical illumination in our world. This passage urges us toward a proactive approach of loving our fellow humans and pursuing the rights of the marginalized (see also Isaiah 1:17). The prevailing idea of this book is that politics is a compelling platform for Christians to respond to this scriptural call.

Many times the idea of advocacy and protest is met with suspicion in Christian circles, even among those who desire to engage in the political space. The word *protest* can summon mental images of people who have given up on the system's capacity or desire to render just action, taking to the streets in chaos and violence. And *advocacy* is often seen as the domain of self-seeking interest groups. But protest need not be rooted in incivility, hopelessness, or pride, and advocacy need not be self-centered or mean. In fact, the strategic precision and technical skills required for effective protest and advocacy particularly suit themselves to people with love in their hearts toward God and their fellow humans, a hope rooted in God's ability to make things happen, and a clear and sober mind (2 Timothy 1:7; 1 Peter 4:7).

Protest and Advocacy as a Platform for Christian Engagement

What is protest? What is advocacy? The two certainly go hand in hand, but in order to use these two important skills, we have to distinguish between them.

Protest is publicly registering disapproval of some action or set of circumstances for the purpose of moving those with power to act. *Advocacy* can be private or public and can register disapproval of some action or policy, positively express support for a particular approach to a problem, or both. An easy way to think about it is that *advocacy* is the large body of work done to make sure that political decision makers make the right decisions. *Protest* is what is done in order to let them know when they have made the wrong decision.

One of the effects that Christ has had on our spiritual nature is what the apostle Paul calls a zeal for "good works" (Titus 2:14 ESV). When Christians see something wrong or broken in our world, there is a desire on the inside—a desire emanating from the Spirit of God in us—that makes us want to do something about it. The Christian heart cannot easily tolerate the sight of people going to bed hungry. We don't embrace the reality of people made in the image of God being deprived of basic human dignity. Christians want to help people.

One response to this Christian desire to alleviate human suffering is direct help. In efforts to work against poverty, we might personally provide food to the hungry or take clothes to people who do not have them. Another valid way to engage might be to empower people to better their own circumstances. For instance, job readiness training represents a slightly different approach to alleviating the scourge of poverty. You've heard the old adage "Give a man a fish, he eats for a day. Teach a man to fish, he eats for a lifetime." But what if there is a law that makes it illegal for that man to fish unless he travels to a town five hundred miles away to receive a fishing license? What if the man had a felony record from a misspent youth, and for that reason he is simply not allowed to fish in the state where he lives? How then will Christians engage?

Protest and advocacy are among the most effective tools that we can use to pursue improvements in the lives of others through the civic/political process. Like a hammer or a chainsaw, protest and advocacy can be wielded to do tremendous good or to cause tremendous harm. But when Christians use these tools to pursue improvements in the lives of hurting people and to uphold eternal values in our society, we effectively love our neighbors and, by way of these good deeds, glorify our Father in heaven (Matthew 5:16).

The Christian's Approach

Passion is what drives a person into the political arena. For the Christian, that passion should be the basic desire to good: to pursue justice and uphold timeless truth. But whether driven by passionate desire for control, passionate greed, or even a more humanistic motivation to help other people, we are hard-pressed to find a political actor without a passion for something or someone. With so many passionate people and interests competing for finite resources and influence in government and civic life, it's no wonder that protest and advocacy often take on some of the horrible images our minds tend to conjure when we hear the words. The political space is uniquely passionate and necessarily competitive, but that does not mean Christians are not able to engage in a way that reflects our values and honors our God.

As Christians our approach to protest and advocacy should reflect the moral light we have been called to. Our political actions should be honest, humble, respectful of human dignity— even of those we disagree with—and free from guile. Other actors in the political space may seem to get ahead through deceit, disrespect, pride, and violence, and this can be discouraging for Christians. But Psalm 73 provides a powerful reminder that even though the wicked may seem to be getting away with things, when we enter "the sanctuary of God" we understand "their final destiny" (Psalm 73:17). In political life, as in all other areas of life, we must reject the evil practices that are in the world because of sin.

Behavior is an outflow of matters of the heart. Spiritual discipline is of the utmost importance for believers who want to engage in protest and advocacy. We have to be dedicated to regular, prayerful self-assessment, asking God to search our hearts and prove our motives. Those engaged in protest and advocacy are particularly susceptible to two temptations: power and offense.

The realm of political engagement is all about the development and use of power. In the political sense power is simply the ability to make things happen in government and civic life.

Political power is not inherently evil, but there is temptation in this area to use the power and influence one develops for mere personal gain. Surely our interests *and* the interests of our communities ought to be represented in our politics. But are we seeking to use our power to look out for the needs of others and to seek their good *above* our own?

Christians should also avoid the temptation in politics to use power and influence to punish our enemies. Neither offense nor hatred should be the impetus for our protests and advocacy. Hatred and bigotry have no place at all in the body of Christ. But even when we suffer legitimate wrongs, we must remember that vengeance belongs to the Lord (Romans 12:19). This doesn't mean that we don't seek to win campaigns or pass legislation, but the motivation for our political activities—particularly protest and advocacy—should always be to help others, never to punish someone.

These are questions of the heart, and they are not easy to answer. But Christians must never assume the best of ourselves. Ours must always be the prayer of Psalm 139:23: "Search me, God."

The Bible on Protest and Advocacy

The Scriptures guide us by precept and example in the areas of protest and advocacy. While there aren't truly democratic forms of government in the Bible, we certainly find examples of both protest and advocacy. The first chapter of this book lays out a solid explanation of the Bible's general counsel on political engagement. But before we look at some biblical examples of protest and advocacy, let's look at one important principle of Scripture as it relates to how Christians interact with government.

One of the most direct instructions we have in Scripture about relating to the government is found in Romans 13:1: "Let everyone be subject to the governing authorities, for there is no authority except that which God has established. The authorities that exist have been established by God."

This may first appear to be a theological challenge to the idea of engaging in protest with the goal of altering the opinions and actions of elected officials and other decision makers. However, a better understanding of our peculiar system of government turns that logic on its head. Our government is a representative democracy. It is government of the people, for the people, and by the people. Through the electoral process, we essentially hire officials to manage our own government. They are managers and servants, but the authority of the government rests ultimately with the people.

The health of our government depends on an informed and rigorously engaged citizenry. Advocacy and protest are the tools we use to manage our elected servants. Because we live in a democracy, Romans 13:1 is not an injunction against protest and advocacy, but a mandate for it.

The Bible offers some compelling examples of protest and advocacy. Keep in mind that these accounts took place under materially different forms of government than our democratic republic, and we must carefully consider how the principles they demonstrate apply in our own times. Nonetheless, these biblical examples of protest and advocacy can give us some ideas about how to design our efforts. More important, these examples show us that the tools of advocacy and protest are tools God's people can use to faithfully engage in the project of self-governance.

BIBLICAL EXAMPLES OF PROTEST

Shadrach, Meshach, and Abednego *(Daniel 3)*

When the nation of Israel was in captivity in Babylon, King Nebuchadnezzar chose several of his captives to be advisers in his court. While at first these servants of God found peaceable ways to exist in the Babylonian court, the king made a decree that asked them to violate the First Commandment (to worship the Lord alone). The king decreed that at the sound of music, all of the members of his court had to bow down and worship a golden image the king had made. Shadrach, Meshach, and Abednego met this unrighteous law with a protest; they refused to bow to the golden image. These young men courageously faced the legal consequences of their protest, being thrown in a fiery furnace. The Lord delivered the Hebrew boys by a miracle, but the entire chain of events was catalyzed by a courageous protest.

Jesus Cleanses the Temple *(John 2:13-17)*

During Jesus' ministry on the earth, he went to Jerusalem for Passover as was his custom. When he arrived at the temple, he saw money changers "doing business." This merchandising dishonored the house of God, and Jesus knew it. Jesus' tactical approach was that he made a whip from cords and began to chase the money changers and the animals they were selling out of the temple. He also overturned the tables they were using to count the money. This protest caused quite a scene, but Jesus did not hurt anyone or violate any laws. In fact, the demonstration highlighted the need for the people to move in the direction of righteousness.

Jesus Protects the Woman Caught in Sin *(John 8:1-11)*

Once while Jesus was teaching a group, Pharisees brought him a woman caught in adultery. They made the accusation that she was caught in the very act. They articulated for Jesus (as if he didn't know) that the law instructed them to stone the woman to death. Just when the Pharisees thought they had trapped Jesus in a legal quandary, he stooped down and engaged in a demonstration. He wrote something in the dirt of the ground with his finger. He then stood up and said, "Let any one of you who is without sin be the first to throw a stone at her." Then he knelt again and continued to write. Perhaps Jesus was writing the sins of the Pharisees in the dirt. Whatever it was, the combination of Jesus' words and his writing was an effective protest that influenced the Pharisees, but it was also meaningful advocacy on behalf of the woman. One by one, the Pharisees dropped their stones and walked away.

BIBLICAL EXAMPLES OF ADVOCACY

Moses and Aaron Speak to Pharaoh (Exodus 5–12)

The interactions between Moses, Aaron, and Pharaoh are perhaps the greatest example of advocacy in Scripture. God used these two brothers to deliver the nation of Israel from Egyptian bondage. The account of this delivery is a classic case of advocacy. Moses and Aaron presented a policy proposal: allow the people to go into the wilderness and worship the Lord. That would represent a real improvement in the lives of the people—a first step toward the long-term deliverance that God had promised. When Pharaoh refused, what ensued was a continual process of Moses and Aaron lobbying Pharaoh for the release of the people. God worked with Moses and Aaron, sending various plagues that significantly disrupted the comfort of Egyptian life. This is instructive, as the narrative highlights how protest and advocacy work in tandem to win real improvements in people's lives. In the final analysis, the pressure tactics became too much for Pharaoh, and he relented to Moses and Aaron's demand.

Esther Speaks to the King *(Esther 4–5)*
During the reign of King Xerxes in Persia (after the first remnant of Jews had returned to Jerusalem), a Jewish woman named Esther was chosen to become the king's wife and a queen in his domain. In the course of time, one of the king's top advisers, Haman, hatched a genocidal plot to kill all of the Jews remaining in the kingdom. Esther's cousin, Mordecai, learned of the plan and told Esther. Mordecai encouraged Esther that as a queen in the domain, she would be best suited to speak to the king against Haman's evil policy. At significant risk to her own life and safety, Esther agreed to speak to the king on behalf of all the Jews. Through a set of advocacy-oriented conversations, Esther uncovered the plot to King Xerxes and convinced him to reject Haman's policy of genocide.

Thoughts on Effective Strategies and Tactics

Like any other field of endeavor, effective political engagement requires a range of skills, and as Christians we must never make the mistake of thinking that the right motives are a substitute for strategic precision and skill. We can't bring about change if we are not skilled in our practices of protest and advocacy (Proverbs 22:29). It is not enough simply to act; our actions must be effective. There is much more to discuss about developing and implementing effective political protest and advocacy than we have space to cover here, but here are few guiding thoughts that will help Christians on our way.

One of the most critical mistakes that a political actor can make in the domain of protest and advocacy is to act before a strategy is in place. Tactics or actions must always flow out of a well-conceived strategy. Getting this wrong could render our actions ineffective—or worse, do harm to our cause, the community we set out to help, or both.

113

Developing a strategy is different from planning. Planning only involves laying out the steps we will take to accomplish a certain task. For instance, we can plan a protest march or a letter-writing campaign. But effective advocacy has to consider not only our ability to act but also how others will respond to those actions. A strategy is a design of potential actions and reactions based on an analysis of the context and relationships. A good strategy comes from answering the following questions.

PARTNERSHIP STRATEGY QUESTIONS

1. What do we want?

This question clarifies the goals of your efforts. What exactly are you trying to accomplish? The more specific you can be, the better.

Good: End poverty in my city

Better: Make it easier for young people to get jobs

Best: Get $500K in the budget for a youth jobs effort

2. Who is the decision maker?

Who is the decision maker with the ability to give you what you want? Again, be specific.

Good: The city government

Better: The city council

Best: We need eight of these fifteen council members to support our initiative (list their names and analyze each one individually)

3. Who is on the team?

Who are the people who might be willing to help you? Think about all of the potential points of connection.

Good: Direct beneficiaries (e.g., youth looking for work)

Better: Indirect beneficiaries (e.g., parents, employers)

Best: Ideological supporters and tangential beneficiaries (e.g., schools, youth counselors, churches, antiviolence groups)

4. What do we have?

Now that you know your team, what resources can the team bring to the effort? Again, specificity is key.

Good: Money, people, and relationships

Better: Get specific information on budgets, memberships, lists, and relationships

Best: Get specific commitments from people and organizations about what they are willing to contribute

After these strategy questions have been answered (and only after they have been answered), we can move on to developing tactics. What can *the team* do with *what we have* to get the *decision maker* to give us *what we want?* If we don't know the answers to these strategy questions, there will inevitably be holes in how we think about tactics. Many times protest or advocacy goes nowhere because of this. The following are four rules we should always follow as we develop and implement tactics in protest and advocacy:

1. Focus on the decision maker. If the tactic does not impact the decision maker (at least at the secondary level), you will probably not move the decision maker to support your issue.

2. Highlight your specific goal. Your tactics should highlight what you want, not distract from it.

3. Make sure your team can pull it off. There is no benefit to your community or cause to set out to do something that you will ultimately be unable to do. Before planning an action, make sure you can actually do it (Luke 14:28-30).

4. Your work must disturb the equilibrium. Protest and advocacy have to get noticed to be effective. This does not mean that your tactics should be obnoxious, violent, or inconsiderate. But if business as usual will continue once your action has ended, it is unlikely to spark the change you are trying to bring about.

CHAPTER EIGHT

CIVILITY

POLITICAL CULTURE

Incivility in politics is not new. American politics has always been intertwined with and informed by personal animosities and egos. There have often been issues that roiled the passions of the public and provoked the derogatory or even the violent.

Yet we need not romanticize the past to notice the danger in the present. Something has changed. Social science makes it clear, but even if it didn't, we feel it in our lives.[1] It used to be that we could look at Washington, DC, and our state capitols and think that partisan and political animosities were contained there, but that those places did not reflect "real America." This is no longer possible. Today, partisan antipathy too often motivates people to dehumanize themselves and others on social media and in real life.

Civility is how we treat one another in public, or what philosopher and former president of Fuller Seminary Richard Mouw called "public politeness."[2] It amounts to a set of norms that make up a code of public decency. In politics, civility shows itself in respect for disagreement and in granting others the right to express it. Civility shows itself when we acknowledge the best in our political opponents' line of thinking and the best in our political opponents themselves. Civility is mercy and forgiveness. It is a form of public grace.

Why Civility Matters

Mouw writes,

> To be good citizens, we must learn to move beyond relationships that are based exclusively on familiarity and intimacy. We must learn how to behave among strangers, to treat people with courtesy not because we know them, but simply because we see them as human beings like ourselves. When we learn the skills of citizenship, Aristotle taught, we have begun to flourish in our humanness.[3]

Scripture is replete with instructions regarding the importance of how we speak to and treat others, and the way we comport ourselves in public. Incivility is not justified by incivility—especially not for Christians. Peter instructs believers,

> Do not repay evil with evil or insult with insult. On the contrary, repay evil with blessing, because to this you were called so that you may inherit a blessing. For,

> "Whoever would love life
>   and see good days
> must keep their tongue from evil
>   and their lips from deceitful speech.
> They must turn from evil and do good;
>   they must seek peace and pursue it.
> For the eyes of the Lord are on the righteous
>   and his ears are attentive to their prayer,
> but the face of the Lord is against those who do evil."
>   (1 Peter 3:9-12)

Civility and Human Dignity

Civility is the kind of thing we tend to discuss when it is violated, but it is just as recognizable when it is evident. That is to say, we appreciate civility when it is present, to a similar degree that we miss it when it is absent. This is because civility is a recognition of human dignity. All incivility is, at its root, preceded by dehumanization. Incivility is toxic because it stems from a lapse in the recognition of human dignity: recognition of the dignity of others or recognition of one's own dignity.

In its purest form incivility amounts to public hatred. We must consider what hatred does to the soul of our commonwealth, the soul of our nation, and the souls of our citizens. Howard Thurman, the brilliant theologian and spiritual mentor of Martin Luther King Jr., discusses the roots of hatred in his book *Jesus and the Disinherited*, and his thoughts are relevant here.

Howard Thurman and a Politics of Hate

Howard Thurman believed hate needed to be rooted out of the heart of society, but he also believed that mere sentimentality was not sufficient. According to Thurman, hatred had a cause and rationality that needed to be taken seriously. He described a kind of four-stage process in the development of hate. It often begins, Thurman wrote, "in a situation in which there is contact without fellowship."[4] He explained, "Much of modern life is so impersonal that there is always opportunity for the seeds of hatred to grow unmolested."[5]

Second, Thurman believed that when we are confronted with one another but are never really in a position to *be* with one another, we develop an understanding of the other that is strikingly unsympathetic. We are close enough to people to observe them, but through that shallow contact we develop an understanding of them that is "hard, cold, minute and deadly."[6] Third, this cold understanding—this ugly portrait of our fellow citizen, our fellow man or woman—we form in our minds then tends to express itself "in the active functioning of ill will."[7] And fourth, when that ill will becomes such that it animates a human being, it becomes "hatred walking on earth."[8]

"Contact without fellowship" is a good description of what social science has confirmed as the developing relationship between Americans of different political parties.[9] (Twitter is a good example of contact without fellowship.) We are increasingly self-segregating ideologically, so we don't live in community as neighbors with people who disagree with us politically. We deem shared political allegiances as essential criteria for the spouses our children will marry. We receive media through tailored sources that highlight the worst of our political opponents. All this allows us to develop a cold understanding that breeds ill will.

This kind of hatred is cultivated in our politics today by those who channel hatred for their purposes—because people can be organized based on common hatreds. They can raise money off of promises that others hate the same things and the same people they hate. For those who feel cheated, who feel they have been treated unjustly, Thurman writes, "Every expression of intolerance, every attitude of meanness, every statute that limits and degrades, gives further justification" for hatred.[10]

In our political environment everyone feels under attack. Politicians and our political infrastructure of advocacy groups, corporate interests, highly tailored media outlets, and platform-seeking personalities see to it. We've long rewarded those who are the most skilled at humiliating our political opponents with witty rhetoric or ostracizing them with vicious, often unfair, attacks.

How to Cultivate Civility

We enter the public sphere in order to help people. It is striking how quickly, how easily, how subtly we can slip into treating matters that concern the public into matters that only concern us or our tribe. This is where incivility gains leverage, because we forget that politics is a shared project and instead treat it as a personal enterprise and treat disagreement as a personal affront.

Citizenship calls us to engage differently. Political engagement motivated by service is much more likely to support civility. When we enter into the public square, our goal is not to win but to come alongside our fellow Americans—those in our community—in pursuit of the truth and in pursuit of a shared way forward.

But even here there are pitfalls, so even as we enter the public square to serve, our desire to serve must be tempered by humility about our capacity to serve well, to know what is right, and to know what is actually helpful. A spirit of humility allows us to act without the presumption that we have all the answers and without the burden of needing all the answers before we act.

For Professor John Inazu, humility does not reflect a lack of conviction, but rather reflects

> the limits of translation, and the difficulty of proving our deeply held values to one another. . . . Humility also recognizes that our human faculties are inherently limited—our ability to think, reason and reflect is less than perfect, a limitation that leaves open the possibility that we are wrong.[11]

Incivility often stems from the loss of patience with our neighbors and indignation that they do not yet—and may never—

see the world as we do. Yet patience is often in shorter supply for the zealous convert to a cause than the long-suffering laborer. It is not usually the most vulnerable who are the most vitriolic, nor is it usually they who have persevered for what they believed who are most bitter. Instead, often the people for whom these issues are primarily emotional are trying to prove their commitment rather than just being committed. Those who have advocated for an issue for a long time are able to track progress, are aware of the various points of disagreement, and understand the terrain. Recent converts are often battling self-hatred that it took them so long to "see the light," and they can take that out on those who have yet to see it for themselves. They seem to say, "I've arrived—when will you?"

The truth is, none of us have arrived. Even our well-considered and hard-earned positions can be wrong. They might have unintended consequences and might not achieve what we desperately want to achieve. We might come to realize that our aims have not been set on the right target. Humility helps us separate a person's thinking from their dignity and to recognize and respect the latter even when we vehemently disagree with the former.

Civility Grounded in Hope

Martin Luther King Jr. and other civil rights leaders prepared a document for those who would be participating in the Montgomery, Alabama, bus demonstrations. In anticipation of a Supreme Court mandate ordering the integration of buses, King, then president of the Montgomery Improvement Association, suggested this would "place upon us all a tremendous responsibility of maintaining, in face of what could be some unpleasantness, a calm and loving dignity befitting good citizens."[12] The document goes on to make general recommendations, like "not all white people are opposed to integrated buses. Accept goodwill on the part of many;""in all things observe ordinary rules of courtesy and good behavior;" "be quiet, but friendly; proud, but not arrogant; joyful, but not boisterous;" and "be loving enough to absorb evil, and understanding enough to turn an enemy into a friend."[13]

This document is both inspiring and daunting because civility is both inspiring and daunting. Civility is impossible without a commitment to deeper things than self-interest and the besting of our opponents. At the same time, civility is not passivity toward concrete outcomes. King's faith and confidence in Jesus and in justice that was the will and providence of God allowed him to ground his activism—his political engagement—in strong moral commitments.

In the face of great injustice, civility seems impractical. Yet we should be careful before we discard it. We might find that what we could accomplish with incivility is much better accomplished with civility, and that once civility is discarded it is very difficult to reinstitute.

The Misuse of Civility

Unfortunately, civility is often used as misdirection. Incivility is not an excuse to deflect on issues of public import. And when civility is used as a way to silence ideological opponents, it does nothing but promote cynicism and ultimately undermine civility itself. We should reflect on whether we employ calls for civility in circumstances that might hinder our political ambitions, or whether we only call for civility from those we disagree with.

We should commit to civility in our own behavior and then hold our political allies to a standard of civility. Only after we've done that should we consider it appropriate to request the same from political opponents. Civility should never be used solely or even primarily as a standard we place on those we disagree with. Calls for civility are not a debate tactic.

If we want to see more civility, we ourselves must be even more emphatic about our support for sound democratic processes and a fair, impartial government. Injustice does not justify incivility, but it is reasonable for incivility to spring forth from injustice. People who are proponents of civility but quietists on everything else are, in fact, a great threat to civility. They are silent on voter disenfranchisement, but quick to urge the disenfranchised to be civil in how they express their disagreement. They are silent on the inequities and injustices in our criminal justice system, but are more than happy to retweet videos of protesters blocking highways or cursing at pedestrians. We can hardly encourage civility if we undermine a healthy civic life.

By How We Love One Another: Civility as Christian Witness

Incivility is a public problem, but incivility among Christians in the public square is a genuine threat to the witness of the church. Remember Jesus' prayer in the upper room:

> I pray also for those who will believe in me through their message, that all of them may be one, Father, just as you are in me and I am in you. May they also be in us so that the world may believe that you have sent me. I have given them the glory that you gave me, that they may be one as we are one—I in them and you in me—so that they may

be brought to complete unity. Then the world will know that you sent me and have loved them even as you have loved me. (John 17:20-23)

Christians can be one while disagreeing on prudential policy matters, but we cannot be one while expressing contempt for one another in the public square. We have heard of relationships between Christians fracturing due to political circumstances. We have even heard reports of people physically fighting in church after Trump was elected.

Our responsibility to one another as Christians rises above civility. Civility is the baseline for how we treat strangers, yet no Christian is a stranger to us but is, instead, our brother or sister in Christ. Christians will have political disagreements, too, but our disagreements are to be in the context of mutual love and submission to Christ.

There is wisdom in Paul's admonition in Galatians:

You, my brothers and sisters, were called to be free. But do not use your freedom to indulge the flesh; rather, serve one another humbly in love. For the entire law is fulfilled in keeping this one command: "Love your neighbor as yourself." If you bite and devour each other, watch out or you will be destroyed by each other. (Galatians 5:13-15)

GUIDELINES FOR CIVIL POLITICAL ENGAGEMENT

Civility in disagreement can be supported by a range of practices or guidelines, including the following:

1. Hold out hope for political opponents' best possible motives.

We ought to ascribe the best motives possible to our political opponents, given the information at hand, and do our best to separate intent from impact. Political debates are often about benefits and harms, and we must be free to argue that a particular policy will harm a particular group or sector; this is not slander, nor is it uncivil so long as it is honest. Slander is when we move from arguing about effects to arguing about intent, which is a way to undermine the standing of those we are arguing with in the public square. When we make accusations about their intent, we are in fact saying, "We don't have to pay attention to the substance of their argument because their motivations disqualify them." Sometimes, ill intent will be made clear, and then we must simply state the facts. But where there is reasonable room to offer the benefit of the doubt, we should offer it.

2. Affirm the true and the good in our opponents' argument.

Even when we vehemently disagree with what someone is arguing, try to affirm what is worthy of affirmation. This can help establish common ground, and it explicitly limits the scope of disagreement, which is a buffer against contempt.

3. Avoid deception and manipulation.

Civility requires that we not cheat when we enter the public square, even in the name of what we perceive to be the common good. There are some tools in the political toolbox that civility requires we never use, and deception and manipulation are among them. (See chapter three on rhetoric for more on this point.)

4. Ground political engagement in service.
If our political involvement is motivated by service rather than self-aggrandizement, the pursuit of power, or antipathy, civility will be much more likely. Remember that we enter the public square not to win but to serve. Civility makes the politics of service more habitual.

A CLOSING
EXHORTATION

C hristians can and should enter the public space and actively engage in politics and civics. We've discussed practical paradigms, tools, and tips to make that engagement meaningful and true. But as we set out to labor in the mission field of government, politics, and civic engagement, we must remember that as believers we do not go out alone. The gospel does not simply inform our engagement—the gospel empowers our engagement.

Believers need not be shy about the fact that we bring to this work a unique set of advantages granted to us by the divine power of our living God (2 Peter 1:3). We do not enter this space simply to pursue our own interests but to seek the good of others. We enter the space in order to pursue God's agenda, and when we do that, God adds special grace to our efforts. Because our hearts and minds are fixed on the kingdom of God, we have access to the "great and precious promises" of the Almighty and "may participate in the divine nature" (2 Peter 1:4). It is our sacred responsibility to labor in the name of the Lord. And it is our humble privilege to labor in his power.

In the apostle Paul's second letter to the Corinthians he writes to the church about how best to interact with the culture in light of their faith in Jesus. Near the close of Paul's instructions we receive these wise words: "Whatever you do, do it all for the glory of God" (1 Corinthians 10:31). These words are filled with power. We end our book by echoing Paul's exhortation to the civically and politically engaged Christian; we pray that these words go with you, carried like a treasure in your heart every single day. If you are going to get involved, do it for the glory of God.

Dear Christian, if you are going to do civics and politics, we first urge you to *do it*. All throughout Scripture there are diverse action commands. Without doubt, civic and political engagement begins with what we think and what we believe—and our prayer is that this book has helped to shape and clarify your thinking and belief. But never be drawn off into the false assumption that right thinking and right belief are sufficient. As with so many other areas of this Christian life, orthodoxy is hollow apart from orthopraxy. Christian faith starts with what we think and believe, but it manifests itself in what we do. Democracy is not ultimately an adjective or even a noun; democracy is a verb.

We want you to come away from your time in these pages with a thoroughly biblical understanding of civic and political engagement. But like James, the Lord's brother, we say, "Show me what you believe apart from what you do, and I will show you what I believe by what I do" (see James 2:18). There are many ways to get involved with civic and political life, but one thing they all have in common is that involvement will not only rest on what we think or believe but also on what we have the fortitude to do. Find a place to be engaged, and then jump in the fray.

All civic and political engagement (especially if it is going to be effective and long-term) must be rooted in a clear and compelling *why*. The *why* is the great purpose that drives a person to think critically, speak clearly, act boldly, and endure the challenges inherent to the beautiful mess that is government in a democratic society. First Corinthians 10:31 gives the Christian a *why* that is profoundly clear and remarkably sustaining: we engage in politics to glorify God.

Our purpose in civic engagement is not to make our own names great but to make known the greatness of the One who sends us. Our great desire is to be agents of the will of God in the earth, distribution centers for the love of God toward his creation. The only way we can ever get it right is to keep the admonition in Scripture to put to death the misdeeds of the body with all of its desires for selfish gain.

This *why* is unique among motivations for engagement in that the motivation itself carries with it access to a divine source of power. Whenever we set our hearts to pursue the glory of God, God directs grace to us. First Peter 4:10-11 tells us that we have been given gifts from God that are to be used to serve one another. We also learn here that the high purpose of that service is so that "in everything God may be glorified through Jesus Christ" (ESV). God gets the glory. We get the grace.

This grace cannot be overestimated. It is this divine power that has carried Christians in public service throughout the generations. William Wilberforce was praying for grace when he said, "O Lord, reassure me with Your quickening Spirit; without You I can do nothing."[1] Harriet Tubman called down grace each night when she prayed, "I'm going to hold steady on You, an' You've got to see me through."[2] In his sermon "A Knock at Midnight," Martin Luther King Jr. related a story of the time when the city of Montgomery was sued in court to end the bus boycott.

At our regular weekly mass meeting, scheduled the night before the hearing, I had the responsibility of warning the people that the car pool would probably be enjoined. I knew that they had willingly suffered for nearly twelve months, but could we now ask them to walk back and forth to their jobs? And if not, would we be forced to admit that the protest had failed? For the first time I almost shrank from appearing before them. When the evening came, I mustered sufficient courage to tell them the truth. I tried, however, to conclude on a note of hope. "We have moved all of these months," I said, "in the daring faith that God is with us in our struggle. The many experiences of days gone by have vindicated that faith in a marvelous way. Tonight we must believe that a way will be made out of no way."[3]

The very day that the case was argued in court, the United States Supreme Court ruled that bus segregation is unconstitutional. Someone might suggest that this was the result of artful campaign planning or even mere coincidence. But the best explanation was that God made a way "out of no way." One of the people in the back of that courtroom yelled it out from a faithful heart engaged in a civic struggle for justice, "God Almighty has spoken from Washington."[4]

Christian political and civic engagement is a spiritual offering. It is offering time, talent, and resources to the Lord so he can accomplish his will. When we make such an offering, we can rest assured that the Spirit of God will encourage, animate, activate, protect, guide, and carry us. Indeed, God is able to make all grace abound toward us so that we always have all sufficiency in every good work (2 Corinthians 9:8). As we labor in civics and government, we must never forget that our *why* is not only our motivation but also a source of divine power.

So get out there, believer. Go to your local county. Go to your national party. Go vote—or go register others to vote. Go protest injustice or advocate on behalf of the vulnerable. Go join an organization. Go organize an association. Go create policies or support policymakers. Go run for elected office or go hold elected officials accountable. Go do whatever God puts on your heart to do in our civic and political world. And whatever you do, do it all for the glory of God.

DISCUSSION QUESTIONS

EXERCISES

Chapter One: Christians (&) Politics

Questions

1. Which of the reasons given in this chapter for Christians to engage in the political arena are most inspiring for you? Are any challenging or confusing?

2. How are the Great Commandment (Matthew 22:36-40) and the Great Requirement (Micah 6:8) connected to political engagement?

3. Should political or social change be the primary objective of the Christian life? Why or why not?

4. How have Christians throughout history used political means to do great work for God? Provide three examples.

5. How has Christian political engagement failed or been unfaithful in the past?

Exercise

Divide the group into smaller groups, and have them discuss what actions, activities, and policies Christians should support to improve how society handles each of the following categories. Then have each group choose a representative to present their thoughts to the others.

- Poverty
- Criminal justice
- Religious freedom
- Education

Chapter Two: Church (&) State

Questions

1. How do you respond to the idea that God ordained government as an institution? Which of the biblical purposes for government have been easy for you to see? Which have been difficult for you to see?

2. What does the separation between church and state mean? How is that concept misrepresented?

3. How should Christians respond when government violates human dignity?

4. Why shouldn't Christians force nonbelievers to agree with us through public policy? Ideally, what should happen when we disagree?

Exercise

Separate your class into small groups and have each group list a few ways that politics and policy influence each of the following topics, and discuss it with the class.

- Food
- Paychecks/salaries
- Subjects taught in school
- Parental rights
- Churches

Chapter Three: Compassion (&) Conviction

Questions

1. What reasons does this chapter give for why no one makes political decisions from a completely neutral position? What other reasons can you think of?

2. How do the love and truth, compassion and conviction of the gospel help Christians frame our political engagement?

3. What does it look like for Christians to disagree on political issues and still be faithful?

4. Is it possible to love someone and not affirm or agree with their behavior or lifestyle? Why or why not?

5. Where do conservatives tend to fall short of the gospel-centered framework for engagement? Where do progressives tend to fall short of this framework?

Exercise

The objective of a Crux Session is to get to the heart of social and political issues. For Christians this involves understanding how the issue should be approached or assessed through a biblical worldview. We're seeking to understand how to apply the truth and love of the gospel to matters we're confronted with in the public square. We'll be fleshing out where Christians should stand on those issues.

The basis for this approach is Ephesians 4, which teaches us about the importance of Christian unity and how we gain understanding and maturity in the body of Christ through group interactions rather than as individuals (Ephesians 4:11-13). The Scripture explains that as we grow together in Christ, we'll no longer be persuaded by the world's teaching, cunning, and scheming. Once mature, we'll be able to speak the truth in love and be more Christlike (Ephesians 4:14-15).

The following points are the rules of engagement for the exercise:

1. The facilitator will bring up a social or political issue and ask someone in the session, "Where's the love?" or tell them to "Kick the truth." (Since biblical love and truth are not mutually exclusive, there may be overlap.)

   a. When asked, "Where's the love?" the person should comment on how Christians should approach the issue based on the kindness and compassion of Jesus Christ.

   b. When told to "Kick the truth," the person should assess the issue based on the moral principles in the Bible.

2. Once the individual has responded, others in the session can respond by saying "Amen" or "Hold up."

   a. When a person responds by saying "Amen," they then must defend the initial person's statement or provide positive feedback.

   b. When a person responds by saying "Hold up," they then must refute the initial statement or add nuance.

3. Dialogue must be civil.

4. No hypersensitivity is allowed: this is not a politically correct zone. We want everyone to be able to speak their minds openly without fear of being policed or criticized for not using the perfect terms. The conversation needs to be civil, but our sensitivities shouldn't be used to silence our opposition or keep others from critiquing our arguments.

5. Participants can't use buzzwords or catchphrases to make their point. These terms are often used as shortcuts, and they

keep us from thoroughly thinking through the issues and our own assumptions. If someone uses one of these terms, the moderator should make them explain what exactly they mean.

Chapter Four: Partnerships (&) Partisanship

Questions

1. How would you express the potential for Christians to partner with nonbelievers to pursue God's will and improve the lives of others? What ways have you seen this work, or can you envision this happening?

2. Why is it important for Christians to understand their partners' value system and their short- and long-term objectives? What are some examples of Christians failing to do this?

3. What's the difference between a cobelligerent and a partner according to Francis Schaeffer?

4. Why can't Christians allow themselves to be indoctrinated by political parties or ideological tribes?

5. Why must Christians vocally critique and challenge political parties and other partners?

Exercise

Form small groups and evaluate each of the following organizations. If you're not familiar with the organization, have one of the small group members look it up. Write out answers to the following:

1. What values and objectives might a Christian share with the group?

2. What might be conflicting values between a Christian and the group?

3. What is your general critique of the groups below based on the biblical framework provided in chapter three?

- ■ American Civil Liberties Union
- ■ Americans for Prosperity
- ■ Black Lives Matter

Chapter Five: Messaging (&) Rhetoric

Questions

1. Why is messaging so important to Christians?

2. How do we see messaging used in the Old Testament and the New Testament? Provide examples.

3. Provide three examples of deceptive messages in politics.

4. How is political messaging used to reduce important issues?

5. How can labeling our political opponents cause us to dehumanize them?

6. List three Scriptures that instruct us in relation to how we should communicate with our neighbors.

Exercise

Print out four or five political opinion articles written about controversial subjects. Separate your class into groups so that each group has an article. Ask each group to review its article and circle any potentially ambiguous or deceptive words or phrases. Then have the group discuss how the use of the word or phrase could be deceptive to readers or harmful to the overall issue. Have each group share its findings with the class.

Chapter Six: Politics (&) Race

Questions

1. See Acts 6; 19; and Galatians 2. How are these situations of racial injustice like those faced in the American church today? How are they unlike them?

2. Describe in your own words the impetus for the founding of the African Methodist Episcopal Church.

3. What does the word *colorblind* used in discussions of race mean to you? What does the chapter suggest are the negative byproducts of a colorblind ideology? What others can you think of?

4. How did American racism create identity politics?

5. How can identity politics be harmful to our political landscape?

6. How can Christians make sure that we avoid mob mentality and take a more thoughtful approach to engagement?

Exercise

The chapter lays out four phases of racial reconciliation as it can be pursued in the context of civic engagement. Where is your congregation or group on the continuum? In groups, brainstorm an engagement that your local body could actually do to take the next step toward reconciled engagement with a racially or ethnically different group of people.

Chapter Seven: Advocacy (&) Protest

Questions

1. How does the Matthew 5 concept of Christians being "salt and light" speak to our ability and willingness to engage in protest and advocacy?

2. What is the distinction between advocacy and protest? What examples come to mind from the reading and your experience?

3. What psalm contains a helpful meditation for Christians who desire to keep their hearts from envy toward the seeming effectiveness of political bad actors?

4. How does it speak to you?

5. Name one biblical example of protest and one biblical example of advocacy.

6. Can you think of others?

7. Why is it important to answer the "strategy questions" before you plan tactics?

Exercise

Arrange the class into groups. Assign each group a scenario from the following list (or feel free to create more locally relevant scenarios modeled from these examples). Have each group answer the "strategy questions" and then list two to three tactics for protest, advocacy, or both that they might pursue.

Scenario 1: School Board Updating Sex Education Policy

The local school board has received a proposal from district staff to update the sex education policy to include about "alternative family structures, including same-sex parents" in the third-through twelfth-grade curriculum (with appropriate information presented at each grade level). The seven elected board members are expected to vote on acceptance or rejection of this proposal at the regular meeting three months from now.

Scenario 2: Police Accountability

A police officer in a small suburban community has shot and killed a young African American security guard who was trying to break up a fight outside of a nightclub where he was working. The police officer has reported in a written statement that the young man pointed a gun at him. But witnesses say that the report is false. The police chief has decided to run an internal investigation of the matter through regular channels. But your clergy coalition feels that a third-party investigation should be conducted.

Scenario 3: Congressman to Vote on Equality Act

A bill that would strike an effective balance between religious liberty and the need to protect LGBTQ people from discrimination in important areas like housing and employment has reached a floor vote in the state legislature. Your legislator is under tremendous pressure from groups on the extreme wing of her political party to oppose the bill. But your church and many other church groups want her to support it.

Scenario 4: Railroad Displacing Community Members

A large national railroad company wants to build a new freight hub in a low-income neighborhood in your city. The company has already acquired all of the land surrounding a group of about 120 homes from the city through a closed-door deal with local officials. Now they are waging a misinformation campaign to homeowners (many of them elderly) telling them that they will soon lose their homes to eminent domain as a way to get the homeowners to sell to the railroad at below-market prices and without any support or funds for relocation. You are a part of a network of faith leaders who want to support these homeowners to either keep their homes or receive sufficient compensation to relocate comfortably.

Chapter Eight: Civility (&) Political Culture

Questions

1. How would you define civility?

2. How can hope ground and motivate civility?

3. How does hope make civility more possible?

4. What do you think of the idea that incivility, in its worst expressions, can amount to a form of public hate?

5. Why is incivility a poor fit for a public witness oriented toward love of God and love of neighbor?

6. Do you find it more difficult to be civil in political disagreements with strangers, or with those you know well?

Exercise

Look at the website of a major news publication (*New York Times, Wall Street Journal, Washington Post*) and find examples of incivility. Discuss these examples with your group. Does incivility seem constructive or destructive? Are there alternative ways you could envision approaching the situation that would put into practice what you've learned in this curriculum while holding to basic civility?

NOTES

1. Christians (&) Politics

[1]Caryl-Sue Micalizio and National Geographic Society, "May 28, 1830 CE: Indian Removal Act," *Resource Library: This Day in Geographic History*, National Geographic Society, April 30, 2014, www.nationalgeographic.org /thisday/may28/indian-removal-act.

[2]Robert L. Burgdorf, "Why I Wrote the Americans with Disabilities Act," *Washington Post*, July 24, 2005, www.washingtonpost.com/posteverything /wp/2015/07/24/why-the-americans-with-disabilities-act-mattered.

[3]Equal Opportunity for Individuals with Disabilities Act of 1990, 42 U.S.C. § 12101 (2009), www.govinfo.gov/content/pkg/USCODE-2009-title42 /html/USCODE-2009-title42-chap126.htm.

2. Church (&) State

[1]Michael Gerson and Peter Wehner, *City of Man: Religion and Politics in a New Era* (Chicago: Moody Publishers, 2010), 92.

[2]Institute for Economics & Peace, *Global Peace Index 2019: Measuring Peace in a Complex World* (Sydney: Vision of Humanity, 2019), http://visionof humanity.org/app/uploads/2019/07/GPI-2019web.pdf.

[3]Abraham Lincoln, "Gettysburg Address," Voices of Democracy: The U.S. Oratory Project, www.voicesofdemocracy.umd.edu/lincoln-gettysburg-address -speech-text.

[4]Lemon v. Kurtzman, 403 U.S. 602 (1971).

[5]Prince v. Massachusetts, 321 U.S. 158 (1944).

[6]Howard Thurman, *Jesus and the Disinherited* (Boston: Beacon Press, 1996); and Kira Dault, "What Is the Preferential Option for the Poor?" *U.S. Catholic* 80, no. 1 (January 2015): 46, www.uscatholic.org/articles/201501/what-preferential -option-poor-29649.

[7]American Sociological Association, "Beginning Pornography Use Associated with Increase in Probability of Divorce," *ScienceDaily*, August 22, 2016, www.sciencedaily.com/releases/2016/08/160822083354.htm.

[8]John Inazu, *Confident Pluralism: Surviving and Thriving Through Deep Difference* (Chicago: University of Chicago Press, 2016), 85.

3. Compassion (&) Conviction

[1]Timothy Keller, *The Meaning of Marriage* (New York: Penguin, 2011), 40.

[2]Upton Sinclair, *The Jungle* (New York: Penguin, 1985).

[3]Jonah Goldberg, "Lott Lesson," *National Review*, December 20, 2002, www.nationalreview.com/2002/12/lott-lesson-jonah-goldberg.

4. Partnerships (&) Partisanship

[1]Jeff Greenstein, "When Richard Nixon Used Billy Graham," *Politico*, February 21, 2018, www.politico.com/magazine/story/2018/02/21/billy-graham-death-richard-nixon-217039.

[2]Greenstein, "Richard Nixon."

[3]Aristotle, *Politics* (Oxford, UK: Clarendon Press, 1905).

[4]Francis Schaeffer, quoted in Colin Duriez, *Francis Schaeffer: An Authentic Life* (Wheaton, IL: Crossway, 2008), 192.

[5]Schaeffer, quoted in Duriez, *Francis Schaeffer*, 192.

[6]"Freedom Riders," *PBS American Experience*, season 23, episode 12, directed and written by Stanley Nelson, aired May 16, 2011.

[7]"Freedom Riders."

[8]"Party Affiliation," *Gallup*, accessed November 18, 2019, https://news.gallup.com/poll/15370/party-affiliation.aspx.

[9]Stephen Hawkins, Daniel Yudkin, Míriam Juan-Torres, and Tom Dixon, "The Hidden Tribes of America," More in Common, accessed November 18, 2019, https://hiddentribes.us.

[10]Hawkins et al., "Hidden Tribes."

[11]Hawkins et al., "Hidden Tribes."

[12]Hawkins et al., "Hidden Tribes."

[13]"Mozilla CEO Resignation Raises Free Speech Issues," *USA Today*, April 4, 2014, www.usatoday.com/story/news/nation/2014/04/04/mozilla-ceo-resignation-free-speech/7328759.

[14]Hamil Harris, "Donnie McClurkin Withdraws from March on Washington Commemoration Concert," *Washington Post*, August 11, 2013, www.washing

tonpost.com/local/donnie-mcclurkin-withdraws-from-king-memorial-con
cert/2013/08/10/3782b804-0202-11e3-9711-3708310f6f4d_story.html.

[15]In a statement released on her website (https://sarahforgeorgia.com/), Sarah
Riggs said, "Although I attend an Evangelical Christian church, I have
always been vocal in my disagreement with their anti-LGBTQ stances. I am
not afraid to stand up for what is right;" also see Patrick Saunders, "Sarah
Riggs Amico Touts Faith, LGBTQ Equality in Lt. Gov Run," *Project Q
Atlanta*, August 7, 2018, www.projectq.us/atlanta/sarah_riggs_amico_touts
_faith_lgbtq_equality_lieutenant_governor_run?gid=19149.

[16]Caitlin Flanagan, "Losing the *Rare* in 'Safe, Legal, and Rare,'" *Atlantic*, December 6, 2019, www.theatlantic.com/ideas/archive/2019/12/the-brilliance
-of-safe-legal-and-rare/603151.

[17]Frederick Douglass, *The Anti-Slavery Movement: A Lecture by Frederick
Douglass Before the Rochester Ladies' Anti-Slavery Society* (Rochester, NY: Lee,
Mann, 1855), 33.

[18]Douglass, *Anti-Slavery Movement.*

5. Messaging (&) Rhetoric

[1]Franklin Delano Roosevelt, "First Inaugural Address," *Avalon Project*, accessed
December 3, 2019, https://avalon.law.yale.edu/20th_century/froos1.asp.

[2]Richard Burke, "Politics as Rhetoric," *Ethics* 93, no. 1 (October 1982): 45.

[3]Greg Forster, *Joy for the World: How Christianity Lost Its Cultural Influence
and Can Begin Rebuilding It* (Wheaton, IL: Crossway, 2014), 13-15.

[4]Joshua Mark, "Agora," *Ancient History Encyclopedia*, September 2, 2009,
www.ancient.eu/agora.

[5]Tim Keller, "Cultural Engagement That Avoids Triumphalism and Accommodation," *Gospel Coalition*, April 18, 2014, www.thegospelcoalition.org
/reviews/cultural-engagement-avoids-triumphalism-accommodation.

[6]Forster, *Joy for the World*, 15.

[7]Forster, *Joy for the World*, 15.

[8]Keller, "Cultural Engagement."

[9]Burwell v. Hobby Lobby Stores, Inc., 134 S. Ct. 2751 (2014).

[10]George Orwell, "Politics and the English Language," *Horizon*, April 1946,
www.orwell.ru/library/essays/politics/english/e_polit.

[11]Orwell, "Politics."

[12]Robert H. Ducoffe and Reece B. Bonnie, "Deception in Brand Names,"
Journal of Public Policy and Marketing 6 (1987), 93-103.

[13]Abraham Lincoln, "Second Inaugural Address," Avalon Project, accessed December 4, 2019, https://avalon.law.yale.edu/19th_century/lincoln2.asp.

[14]M. Alex Johnson, "God on the Ballot," *MSNBC*, October 26, 2004, www.nbcnews.com/id/5819171/ns/politics/t/god-ballot.

[15]Emily McFarlan Miller, "Clinton Describes Her 'Activist, Social Justice Faith,' to Baptists," *National Catholic Reporter*, September 9, 2016, www.ncronline.org/news/politics/clinton-describes-her-activist-social-justice-faith-baptists.

[16]Christopher Borrelli, "Reagan Used Her, the Country Hated Her. Decades Later, the Welfare Queen of Chicago Refuses to Go Away," *Chicago Tribune*, June 10, 2019, www.chicagotribune.com/entertainment/ct-ent-welfare-queen-josh-levin-0610-story.html.

[17]Simon S. Montefiore, *Young Stalin* (New York: Vintage, 2008), 51-52.

[18]Kay Mills, *This Little Light of Mine: The Life of Fannie Lou Hamer* (Lexington: University Press of Kentucky, 2017), 17.

6. Politics (&) Race

[1]Paul Harvey, *Through the Storm, Through the Night: A History of African American Christianity* (Lanham, MD: Rowman & Littlefield, 2011), 16.

[2]Richard Fuller and Francis Wayland, *Domestic Slavery Considered as a Scriptural Institution* (New York: L. Colby, 1845), https://babel.hathitrust.org/cgi/ssd?id=nyp.33433075935035;seq=13.

[3]Albert J. Raboteau, *Slave Religion: The "Invisible Institution" in the Antebellum South* (Oxford: Oxford University Press, 1978).

[4]Raboteau, *Slave Religion*, 47-55.

[5]Raboteau, *Slave Religion*, 160-66.

[6]E. Franklin Frazier and C. Eric Lincoln, *The Negro Church in America: The Black Church Since Frazier* (New York: Schocken, 1974), 33; and Richard S. Newman, *Freedom's Prophet: Bishop Richard Allen, the AME Church, and the Black Founding Fathers* (New York: NYU Press, 2009), 59-63.

[7]"2013–2014 Civil Rights Data Collection: A First Look," US Department of Ed Civil Rights Data Collection, rev. October 28, 2016, 16-17, www2.ed.gov/about/offices/list/ocr/docs/2013-14-first-look.pdf.

8. Civility (&) Political Culture

[1]Shanto Iyengar and Sean J. Westwood, "Fear and Loathing Across Party Lines: New Evidence on Party Polarization," Stanford University, June 2014, https://pcl.stanford.edu/research/2014/iyengar-ajps-group-polarization.pdf.

[2]Richard J. Mouw, *Uncommon Decency: Christian Civility in an Uncivil World* (Downers Grove, IL: InterVarsity Press, 2010), 14.

[3]Mouw, *Uncommon Decency*, 15-16.

[4]Howard Thurman, *Jesus and the Disinherited* (Boston: Beacon Press, 1996), 65.

[5]Thurman, *Jesus and the Disinherited*, 66.

[6]Thurman, *Jesus and the Disinherited*, 66.

[7]Thurman, *Jesus and the Disinherited*, 67.

[8]Thurman, *Jesus and the Disinherited*, 68.

[9]Emily Badger and Niraj Chokshi, "How We Became Bitter Political Enemies," *New York Times*, June 15, 2017, www.nytimes.com/2017/06/15/upshot/how-we-became-bitter-political-enemies.html.

[10]Thurman, *Jesus and the Disinherited*, 74.

[11]John Inazu, *Confident Pluralism: Surviving and Thriving Through Deep Difference* (Chicago: University of Chicago Press, 2016), 88.

[12]Martin Luther King Jr. and William J. Powell, "Integrated Bus Suggestions," Martin Luther King Jr. Research and Education Institute, December 19, 1956, https://kinginstitute.stanford.edu/king-papers/documents/integrated-bus-suggestions.

[13]King and Powell, "Integrated Bus Suggestions."

A Closing Exhortation

[1]William Wilberforce, quoted in Trevin Wax, "I Know Not What I Am, But to You I Flee: A Prayer of William Wilberforce," *Gospel Coalition*, September 1, 2013, www.thegospelcoalition.org/blogs/trevin-wax/i-know-not-what-i-am-but-to-you-i-flee-a-prayer-of-william-wilberforce.

[2]Harriet Tubman, quoted in Jean M. Humez, *Harriet Tubman: The Life and the Life Stories* (Madison: University of Wisconsin Press, 2006), 183.

[3]Martin Luther King Jr., "A Knock at Midnight," Martin Luther King Jr. Research and Education Institute at Stanford University, June 11, 1967, https://kinginstitute.stanford.edu/king-papers/documents/knock-midnight.

[4]Michael Eric Dyson, "'God Almighty Has Spoken from Washington, D.C.': American Society and Christian Faith," *DePaul Law Review* 42, no. 1 (Fall 1992): 153.

NOTES TO SIDEBARS

Historical Examples

[a]"Wilberforce, William," *Encyclopaedia Britannica*, last modified September 5, 2019, www.britannica.com/biography/William-Wilberforce.

[b]Frederick Douglass, *Narrative of the Life of Frederick Douglass* (New York: Penguin, 1968).

[c]"Booth, Catherine," *Encyclopaedia Britannica*, last modified September 30, 2019, www.britannica.com/biography/Catherine-Booth.

[d]Dorothy Day, *The Long Loneliness: The Autobiography of Dorothy Day* (New York: HarperOne, 2017).

[e]Kay Mills, *This Little Light of Mine: The Life of Fannie Lou Hamer* (Lexington: University Press of Kentucky, 2007).

Marsh v. Chambers (463 US 783)

[a]The authors would like to acknowledge Kareim Oliphant for his work on this section.

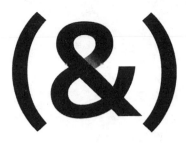

The AND Campaign is a Christian civic organization that asserts the compassion and conviction of the gospel of Jesus Christ into the public square. We believe Christians are called to promote social justice and moral order (rather than one or the other) in the sociopolitical arena, and to transcend both partisanship and political ideology.

The AND Campaign has four primary objectives:

Education: Raise civic literacy among Christians and help believers apply biblical values to the most pressing issues of the day.

Representation: Represent and articulate a clear and credible biblical worldview that Christians can identify with in the public square.

Coalition Building & Reconciliation: Organizing Christians to speak with one voice in the public square, and bridging racial and sociopolitical divides in the church.

Advocacy: Promoting values and policies (i.e., criminal justice, sanctity of life, religious freedom, and voter rights) among policy makers and political decision makers that align with the biblical worldview.

To get involved you can reach out to us at
engage@andcampaign.org
or follow us on social media: @ANDCampaign.